Fashions for Small Dolls

Fashions for Small Dolls

For 7-inch, 8-inch, 9-inch, 10-inch and 12-inch dolls

(18 cm, 20 cm, 23 cm, 25 cm and 31 cm)

Rosemarie Ionker

Reverie

PUBLISHING COMPANY

ACKNOWLEDGMENTS

First, I would like to thank all those who bought my first book, *A Closetful of Doll Clothes*, as this gave me the confidence to start on my second. I should, however, also give my special thanks to Linda Smith, who strongly suggested that I do a book on clothes for small dolls. Without the dolls portrayed in this book, I could not have completed this project, and my thanks, therefore, to all those listed in the chapter "The Dolls in this Book." There would have been no book without the photographs and, again, Tamas Kish provided me with the necessary expert photography. Thanks also to Marilyn Northagen for her suggestions and ideas, as well as Claudia Ionker for her editorial work and the many others not named here who, in one way or another, supported me. Last but not least, I should not fail to mention Thomas Farrell and Krystyna Poray Goddu for their enthusiastic support.

First edition/Second printing

This book was originally published by Portfolio Press Corporation.

To purchase additional copies of this book, please contact:
Reverie Publishing Company, 130 South Wineow Street, Cumberland, MD 21502
888-721-4999 www.reveriepublishing.com

Library of Congress Catalog Card Number 2006929163

ISBN-13: 978-1-932485-33-2
ISBN-10: 1-932485-33-3

Project Editor: Virginia Ann Heyerdahl
Design and Production: Tammy S. Blank
Cover Design: Tammy S. Blank
Cover and Interior Photography: Tamas Kish
Cover doll: Paulinette by Pauline Jacobsen

Printed and bound in Korea

Contents

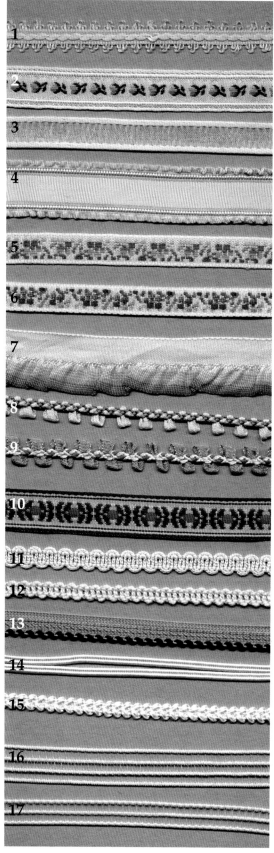

Please turn to page 67 for descriptions of these ribbons.

These delightful dolls
model designs featured in
this book. Note the variety
of sizes and body types

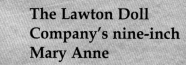

Luna Babies'
nine-inch Rose

The Robert Tonner
Doll Company's
ten-inch Linda

15

This ten-inch boy by
Helen Kish is the
same size as Avery.

Helen Kish's Lauren and Tulah model Rosemarie Ionker's "petticoat dress."

Ten-inch Linda and eight-inch Tulah (center) and Paulinette model their new playsuits.

Helen Kish's
ten-inch Avery
and friend

Opposite page top: Vera
Scholz's nine-inch Christina
Bottom: Jane Davies'
eight-inch Ellie
This page: Robert Tonner's
ten-inch Linda

Erika Catellani's ten-inch dolls model these outfits.

Helen Kish's Tulah and her sister

27

The Lawton Doll
Company's nine-inch
Mary Anne

Helen Kish's
eight-inch Teddy

Eight-inch Ellie and
Paulinette with nine-
inch Rose (sitting)

Christina (left) and Lauren

33

Pauline Jacobsen's
eight-inch Paulinette

35

Seven-inch Cathy, a reproduction of a German doll crafted by Cathy Hansen

Eight-inch Ellie (left) and
Paulinette (right) with nine-
inch Mary Anne

Ten-inch Linda

Avery and her sister

Opposite page, top and bottom:
Heidi, Peter and Linda
This page: Helen Kish's eight-
inch Teddy and ten-inch Avery

Mary Anne (left) and
Avery

Eight-inch Paulinette
and nine-inch Rose

Helen Kish boy and
Vera Schloz's Christina

Seven-inch Molly and
Cathy (shown with her in
the inset photo)

Seven-inch Cathy and
nine-inch Mary Anne

52

Molly and Tulah

The front of the smocked dress with ties attached in the seams which join the side panels to the smocked part.

Back view with the loose back gathered onto the yoke. The width is held with the ties from the front.

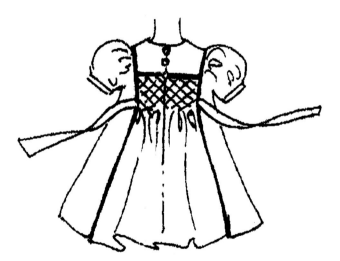

Smocked back which also has ties attached in the seam to tie with the ones from the front on each side under the arm.

Straight back with ties from the front holding the sides and covering the seam in the waist.

Smocking instructions start on page 116.

Getting Started

ℬ ℛ

When I see pictures of small dolls with trunks full of clothing, beautifully made and decorated, I am always fascinated. I marvel at the quality of materials and the time people spent to make these precious little sets. While many of these sets were probably put together by a skillful teacher, mother or grandmother, they were traditionally made to introduce a young girl to sewing and embroidery techniques. I believe that other sets were done by enthusiastic ladies of all ages who loved working with beautiful materials. Imagine all the laces, ribbons and trimmings that were available a hundred years ago! If you could not afford them for your own clothing, at least you had a chance to work with them on these small outfits. Or you might have had little pieces left over — pieces that were just too precious to throw away, but could be put to such good use in dressing small dolls.

A doll with a wardrobe stored in a suitcase or trunk is very popular with present day collectors. The concept of a "Travel doll" has become very fashionable — a little doll that accompanies you on your travels wherever you go. It is a doll that will later remind you of the people and places you visited by the special clothes you made for the occasion. Maybe she has a bridesmaid's dress made for when you take her to the wedding of a friend or relative, a sailor's outfit for the trip to the beach, a folklore dress or "Dirndl" to visit Austria, or a smart coat and dress for a shopping spree in New York. Perhaps she has a special dress to visit a granddaughter's birthday party, or a summer dress with a hat to visit an ice cream parlor. (Does it sound like I am terribly fond of my granddaughter, Sara?) Anyhow, there are millions of reasons to create a new outfit for your little travel companion. This book tries to make the task a little easier, because to make a dress for a small doll is a real challenge.

Maybe you will find more inspiration for your doll dressing dreams within these pages. That is certainly my hope.

The Dolls In This Book

ℬ ℭ

1. Molly, a 7-inch (18 cm) doll by Canadian doll artist Heather Maciak.

2. Cathy, a 7-inch (18 cm) reproduction of a German doll crafted by Cathy Hansen.

3. Tulah, an 8-inch (20 cm) new little doll by Helen Kish.

4. Ginny, an 8-inch (20 cm) doll from The Vogue Doll Company.

5. Ellie, an 8-inch (20 cm) cloth doll designed by Jane Davies.

6. Paulinette, an 8-inch (20 cm) porcelain doll by Pauline Jacobsen.

7. Christina, a 9-inch (23 cm) doll by Vera Scholz. She is only available as a mold.

8. Mary Anne, a 9-inch (23 cm) doll (porcelain head with a wooden body) created by Wendy Lawton to accompany the book *Mary Anne* by Mary Mapes Dodge.

9. Rose, a 9-inch (23 cm) all-porcelain doll from Luna Babies.

10. Avery, a 10-inch (25 cm) vinyl doll by Helen Kish.

11. Linda, a 10-inch (25 cm) vinyl doll from the Robert Tonner Doll Company.

12. Lauren, a 12-inch (31 cm) jointed vinyl doll by Helen Kish.

Also featured in this book are:
Heidi and Peter, 10-inch (25 cm) cloth-bodied dolls with limbs and heads made of wood, crafted by Erika Catellani.

Teddy, an 8-inch (20 cm) vinyl toddler doll by Helen Kish.

"Friends" of Avery and Lauren (who wear the same sizes of clothes) by Helen Kish.

Pattern Notes

ℬ ℭ

While it is, indeed, true that a good deal of skill is required in dressing average-size dolls, it is an even greater challenge to dress small dolls. To make this task a little easier, I have developed a set of patterns that eliminate a few of the most common problems. These patterns have no set-in sleeves, where convex and concave pattern parts have to be connected. This is very difficult to do by machine since the machine foot is often bigger than parts to be sewn together. There are no shoulder seams that would make the little garment bulky. Buttonholes are replaced with thread loops, so that the two parts of the garment are only touching and not overlapping. These are only a few of the problems and their solutions.

The bigger challenge is to determine the size of the pattern to use for a particular doll. Due to the minute differences between the patterns, one has to be extremely careful to determine the right one.

Included here are photographs of all our dolls undressed, to make it easy to see their differences in sizes and proportions.

Molly (No. 1) and Cathy (No. 2) wear the same size clothes, but naturally, Molly needs shorter skirts for a more modern look. Tulah (No. 3) is the same width measurement as Cathy and Molly, which take the pattern for a 7-inch (18 cm) doll. However, you will note Tulah needs her dress length to be that of the pattern for an 8-inch (20 cm) doll.

Ginny (No. 4), Ellie (No. 5) and Paulinette (No. 6) are good girls and wear a proper size 8-inch (20 cm) pattern. The only correction needed is to shorten Ginny's sleeves. Christina (No. 7) is shown here to demonstrate what a doll needing a lengthened size 8-inch (20 cm) pattern would look like.

Mary Anne (No. 8) and Rose (No. 9) both wear a size 9-inch (23 cm) pattern, which fits snugly on Rose whereas the dress hangs a bit more loosely on Mary Anne. Another alteration was to shorten the sleeves for Rose. Avery (No. 10) is a beautiful slim young lady. She wears a lengthened size 9-inch (23 cm) pattern.

Linda (No. 11), one of my most darling little dolls, is an excellent size 10-inch (25 cm) and is such a perfect little thing. In other words, a perfect 10! Lauren (No. 12) is actually taller than the dolls I had planned to use for this book. However, she is a perfect example of a doll that can fit into a lengthened size 10-inch (25cm) pattern. The skirt, sleeves and bodice patterns have to be lengthened for her.

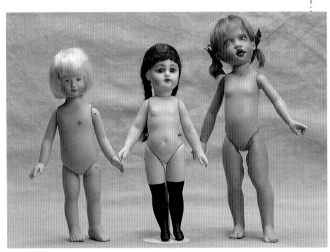

From left: Molly, Cathy and Tulah.

From left: Ginny, Ellie, Paulinette and Christina.

From left: Rose, Mary Anne and Avery.

From left: Linda and Lauren.

Now comes the task of determining what size pattern will be best suited for your doll. With the help of the Dolls Measurement Chart, you can now determine where the dolls you want to dress fit in. Select from the given patterns that which is closest to what you need. Then copy it onto tissue paper and cut out. Glue the pieces together, as a "makeshift" version of the desired clothing item, and place on your doll, adjusting and correcting the pattern accordingly. *Remember that there is a ¼-inch (.6 cm) seam allowance already added to the given patterns.*

Since a basic dress bodice from these patterns has six seams which end at the waist, it is important you are careful to be exact in your work. Otherwise your little dress will not fit properly.

The final pattern has to be drawn onto cardboard to make a template. This eliminates having to pin the pattern pieces onto the fabric. When making the templates for small pattern pieces, it is a good idea to double them, wherever they would be placed on the fold. This is because a fold can easily amount to 1/16 inch (.15 cm) which is a lot on a small garment.

To draw the parts on to the fabric, hold the pattern down and trace around the

Construction of a bodice pattern with shoulder seam

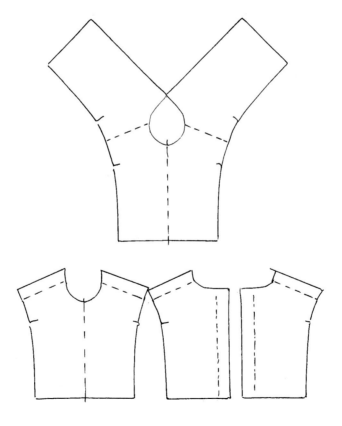

edges with a sharp pencil. The scissors you use to cut these small pieces have to be very sharp in order to cut with the utmost precision. Use the whole blade of the scissors. Do not allow the fabric to slip while cutting a double layer of material since this would cause your parts to be different. Remember that you need to be concerned about every fraction of an inch!

The bodice pattern is constructed in such a way that the center back is in a 135-degree angle to the center front. In this way, both sides of the center back are on the straight grain of the fabric, whereas the center front is on the bias, and vice versa when the dress is opened in front. Because of this, one gets the least distortion after the garment is sewn. The way in which one chooses to construct it should be determined by the material.

If warp and woof is the same, as in batiste and lawn, I prefer to have the front on the bias. In a checked fabric or stripe, it probably looks better to have the front straight. A striped dress with a front opening, like the mariner's dress shown with Erika Catellani ten-inch dolls' wardrobe on page 25, needs to be cut with the stripes going down the center back and meeting in a point in front.

With some materials it is necessary to have shoulder seams so that the sheen of the material is the same in the front and the back. In the case of corduroy, for example, the sheen of the material is quite noticeable. To make a shoulder seam, the bodice pattern is cut across the shoulder, drawn on a new piece of cardboard and ¼ inch (.6 cm) is added to both sides of the shoulder line for the seam allowance, as shown at left.

If properly done, the lining, which is still cut in one piece, will fit inside of the outer fabric that now has a shoulder seam.

The lining for the bodice should be cut in the opposite way as the main material. If the front of the dress material is cut on the bias, then the lining should be straight on the grain in front.

The sleeves: To minimize the chance that the garment looses shape, most of the sleeve patterns are created so that when the center of the sleeve (patterns 3 and 5) is placed on the bias, the part that makes up the side panels of the bodice will be straight on the grain. This way the garment will be less likely to stretch out. Wherever this is not the case (as with pattern 4, or when 3 or 5 cannot be cut on the bias of the fabric), use a small strip of thin — but firm (iron-on) — interlining to strengthen the part that makes up the waistline.

Securing waistline on sleeve parts with interfacing

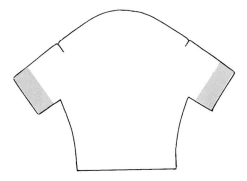

The collars: Collars are best cut with the center back on the bias of the fabric. The lining, which should be cut in the same way, could be a thinner material if the top material is heavier. I do not use interlining for these small collars unless the material is too slippery. In such a case, I may decide against a collar altogether.

The Fabrics

The choice of fabrics for clothing for small dolls can be quite a problem these days. There are only a few suitable fabrics left on the common market. Ideally, only natural fibers should be used, such as cotton, silk and wool; these fabrics are softer and fall better, and they can be steamed and draped to create a more natural appearance in small garments. The fabrics need to be fine and soft but still tightly woven. Since the seam allowances are only ¼ inch (.6 cm), a loosely woven material would fray before the pieces are even sewn together.

Unfortunately, not many fabrics like this are easily available, and it takes a good bit of patience to find what is left on our current markets. Good sources for these are doll shows. You will often find someone there who sells small pieces of unusual materials that are from old stock or especially produced for doll clothes.

The cottons to look for are batiste, muslin, lawn, dimity, liberty cotton, cotton crepe or pinwale corduroy, some fine prints from quilting fabrics and fine cotton linens. Every so often, you can find soft shirting materials in stripes and checks. Coats and jackets for the smallest of dolls can be made from soft cotton satin.

The most suitable silks are tissue taffeta and pongee. Dupion, which is cut across the width of the material, works well also.

The woolen fabrics recommended for suits and winter coats are fine wool crepé, flannel, serge and cashmere.

Another benefit of natural fibers is that they are easy to dye. Therefore, if you do not find the desired colors in a particular fabric, try your hand at dying.

Should you have difficulties in cutting slippery soft fabric, it could be stiffened with starch, preferably an aerosol starch. When using silks, I either double delicate pieces with very fine iron-on batiste interlining, or I secure the seam allowances. My method of securing is to draw a narrow line with a paper-glue dispenser all along the edges of the fabric before cutting. This securing method is more time-consuming because you have to wait until the glue has dried completely before you can continue to work on the piece.

Generally, dolls are best dressed in soft shades of color. Strong colors like reds and blues can be softened by over-dying them with coffee, tea or a textile color of an ecru shade. Try the effect on a small sample of the material first, before deciding what is best. Some of the modern dolls can wear bright colors and even need them to enhance their looks. Robert Tonner's Linda is a good example of this. Does she not look great in her pink coat and hat (page 42)? When I realized this, I created her whole wardrobe around this bright pink coat!

Decorations and Embellishments

ℰ℧   ℭℛ

O f the many ways to decorate, trim and embellish little dresses and outfits, only a limited amount will be applicable for the small sizes with which we will be working.

Laces:

Laces are most important for decorating small garments. The finest is French Valenciennes lace. Make sure to choose those laces where the motif repeats itself most often and use only the narrow ones. I found one edging which I could use to create an *entre deux*. Very narrow edging, such as Valenciennes lace, can be sewn straight to the hem. Otherwise I recommend gathering at least 1½ inches (4 cm) of lace to 1 inch (2.5 cm) of fabric for a wavy look. For more fullness, gather a ratio of 2 inches (5 cm) to 1 inch (2.5 cm) of fabric.

Swiss embroidered laces, featuring small designs on the finest batiste with cotton thread, still can be found at specialty booths at doll shows. Avoid Swiss embroidered laces on coarse cotton and/or embroidered with rayon.

English laces from Nottingham, while done with thicker threads than Valenciennes lace, are interesting to use because of their quick repetition in the design. They almost give the effect of bobbin lace in miniature.

Shown at right:
1 — 11   French Valenciennes lace
12   English cotton lace
13 — 14 Cotton bobbin lace

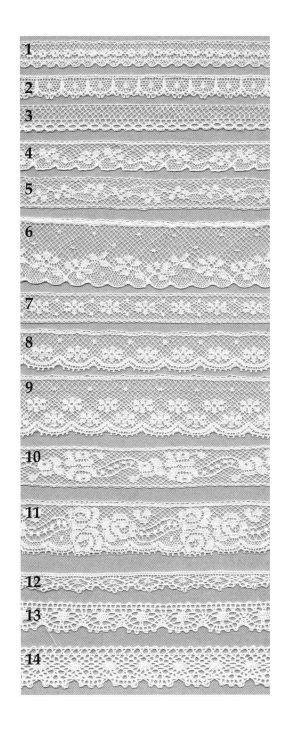

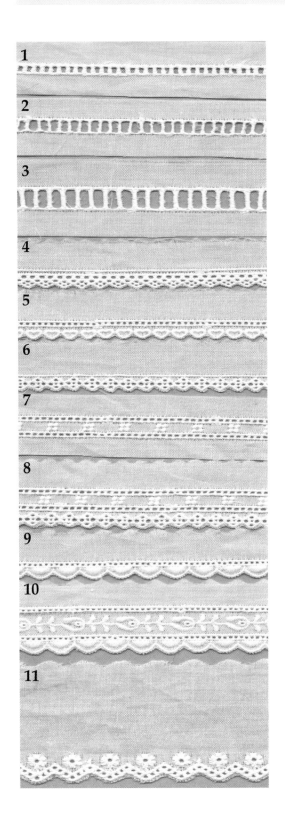

Ribbons:

For our small-sized garments, the ribbons we can use are very limited. The best, of course, are silk ribbons, which are, again, easily found at doll shows. They are produced in Japan and come in 4mm, 7mm and, rarely, in 13mm and 25mm widths.

Alternative to silk are rayon and polyester taffeta ribbons. They come in many plain colors as well as stripes and checks.

French jacquard ribbons, available in several widths, have small flower patterns woven in. Some even have a dainty ruffle on one edge or a ruffled section between the two bands. These ribbons are made of various synthetic fibers like polyester, rayon or acetate. At doll shows, one might even find an old piece of pure silk.

Soutache:

A fine soutache can be used as a simple and easy decoration in straight lines. This is used on antique dolls' clothing in elaborate designs, created by alternately pulling one or the other inner cord of the soutache to form little loops and circles, which are then sewn on by hand. I have never tried this technique on a small garment. I'm afraid that it would look too coarse, because it would be difficult to get all the loops even and to sew them on smoothly. If you want to create the effect of soutache trim in "miniature," try embroidering in chain stitch with two or three threads of floss.

Shown at left:

1 — 3	*Entre deux* embroidered lace
4 — 6	Embroidered edging lace
7	Embroidered *entre deux*
8 — 10	Embroidered edging
11	Embroidered lace

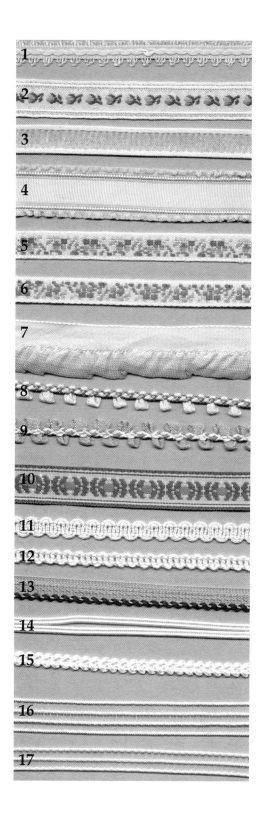

Pearl braid:

I adore pearl braid! It is ideal for accentuating edges. Small collars are easier to finish if they are edged with pearl braid. Corners, however, will take a little practice before you are able to make them look perfect. This is the ultimate trim!

Binding:

This is a way to finish necklines on small garments and is an alternative to cuffs on sleeves. It can be done in a contrasting color to give a special detail to the outfit using a bias band of a suitable material or a special binding braid.

Embroidery:

The most versatile way to decorate small garments is with embroidery. Cotton floss and/or silk ribbons are the ideal materials. Using embroidery along the lines of soutache with either floss or ribbon can soften straight sewn-on soutache. Fine ribbons can be over-embroidered with simple line stitches, such as featherstitch, chain stitch, herringbone or cross-stitch.

At left and shown in color on page 7:

1	French silk braid
2	French flower ribbon
3	French silk ribbon
4	French ribbon with fluted edge
5 & 6	Rayon ribbon
7	Ruffled ribbon
8 & 9	Picot ribbon
10	Flower ribbon
11 & 12	Decorative braid
13	Cording
14	Soutache
15	Pearl braid
16 & 17	Shirring elastic

Edges can be finished with embroidered scallops or picots. A pretty way to fasten hems is with a line of herringbone or chain stitch in all its variations.

If embroidering bigger motifs, remember to do it before the material is cut or even sewn. A good practice is to use an embroidery hoop in order to keep the material under tension and avoid puckering. Even if you prefer not to use a hoop, it is easier to embroider before cutting the material. There is more fabric to hold on to.

When transferring the design that you plan to embroider onto your material, use white or gray transfer paper. If you cannot get this transfer paper, there is another solution, not ideal, but if carefully done, an alternative: Draw your design with a white gel pen onto transparent paper. Turn the paper around and follow these lines on the reverse side with a soft pencil. Now when you trace the design onto the material with a hard tool (tip of a knitting needle or a blunt embroidery needle), the pencil lines will be transferred.

Unfortunately, these will be very soft and need to be redrawn. I generally do this with a fine brush and white or light-gray acrylic paint, because using a pencil often makes smudges. On some materials, a gel pen also works. It is certainly worth trying.

Many of the embroideries will be done on lawn, batiste or other sheer fabrics. In these cases, you place the material onto the embroidery design, making sure to place it straight on the grain. Then carefully copy the lines onto the fabric using a soft pencil or fabric pen.

Smocking:
Smocking is the decorative stitching used to control gathers on loose-fitting traditional shirts, which were called smocks. "Smock" is the old English term for a chemise or shift. Smocks were worn by most agricultural workers and children in England and Wales in the late 17th and 18th centuries. Mechanization rendered the loose-fitting garments impractical and the art of smocking was transferred to decorating ladies' and children's wear. This became very fashionable in the 20th century. During the 1920s and 1930s, it was quite popular for children's clothing to have smocking. Even in our modern times, with the mass production of clothing, the labor-intensive hand-smocking is surviving. Embroidery enthusiasts have developed new ways of using smocking and have documented them in several books on the subject.

For our small dolls, smocking has only limited possibilities. There is so little room on these small bodices to create attractive designs. Despite this, here are some points to consider if you want to experiment with smocking. In order to create a sufficient number of pleats, without jeopardizing the smooth attachment of the yoke, use only thin fabrics. You will need about 32 pleats for every 1 inch (3 cm) on an 8-inch to 9-inch (20 cm to 23 cm) yoke width.

When preparing for smocking, gather the fabric into pleats. On a 10-inch to 11-inch (25 cm to 28 cm) doll's dress, this can be done with the use of transfer dots, which are ironed onto the wrong side of the material and then picked up, row after row, with a needle and strong thread. A commercial smock-gathering machine is faster, but the disadvantage here is that you will be limited to having a certain distance of gathers and fullness of pleats due to the restraint of this machine's capabilities.

For the 9-inch (23 cm) and smaller sizes, the pick-up points should be about 1/8 inch (.31 cm) apart from each other, and one should have about 50 pleats across.

The 7-inch (18 cm) size requires about 44 pleats, the 8-inch (20 cm) size should have about 50 pleats and the 10-inch (25 cm) size needs about 56 pleats.

The gathering rows are used as guidelines for the smocking and, therefore, they need to be accurately straight on the grain of the fabric. Again, for a 10-inch to 11-inch (25 cm to 28 cm) doll, we can remain at a standard distance of 3/8 inch (1 cm) for these rows, but on the smaller sizes, ¼ inch (.6 cm) is recommended.

It is rewarding to use a small checked or striped material (see Ginny's dress, page 54) and it makes gathering so much easier.

When embroidering small dolls' dresses, use only one thread of a six-strand cotton floss. For smocking, use two threads. However, in some cases, such as that of the dress for a 7-inch (18 cm) doll, use only one thread.

All smocking patterns are derived from a few basic stitches that create the multitude of designs in their varied combinations. For small dolls, there is not much combination of stitches possible. Here we are limited to straight rows and the smallest of rhombus designs, which involve four or six pleats per motif. Even with a simple basic design, though, one can create nice effects by filling in the little squares with a variety of flowers or dots in different embroidery stitches.

To hold the shape of the garment tidy and accentuate the dividing line between the smocked panel and the loose skirt, it is useful to do a row of straight smocking on the reverse side, at the lower end of the smocked part. This should be done after all smocking and embroidery is finished.

Pin tucks:
Pin tucks are an easy way to decorate a little dress or pinafore. Using embroidery between the pin tucks will enhance them. If pin tucks are used to decorate a bodice front, be sure to cut a sufficiently large enough piece of material. Determine the distance of the first tuck from the side and mark a straight line following the grain of the fabric. Now, from this first line, mark the number of tucks you will want to make with a fine pencil in even distances across the piece of material. Pin tucks for these small sizes are only about 5/16 inch to 3/8 inch (.75 cm to 1 cm) apart. It is best to make dots instead of a solid line about 2 inches (5 cm) apart. After ironing the pin tucks flat, place the pattern onto the piece of material. Draw the pattern over it and then cut it out. Be sure to get the tucks evenly distanced to the sides of the pattern.

Pin tucks around a hem are done when the hemline is finished. These you can trim with lace or any decorations you find pleasing. The finished hemline is used as a guideline for the tucks. After pressing, trim the skirt to the required length and sew to the bodice.

Embroidery Patterns

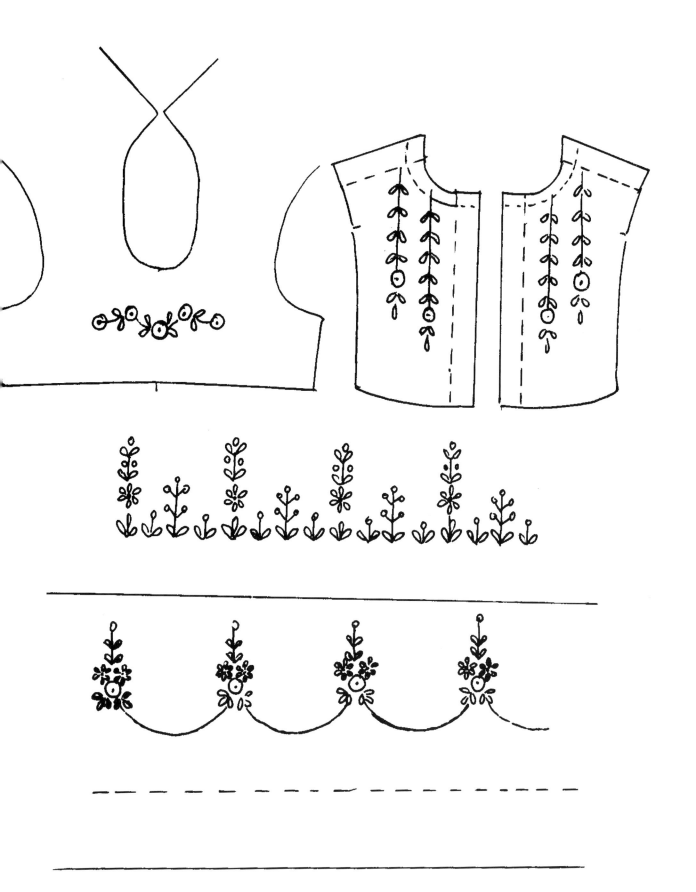

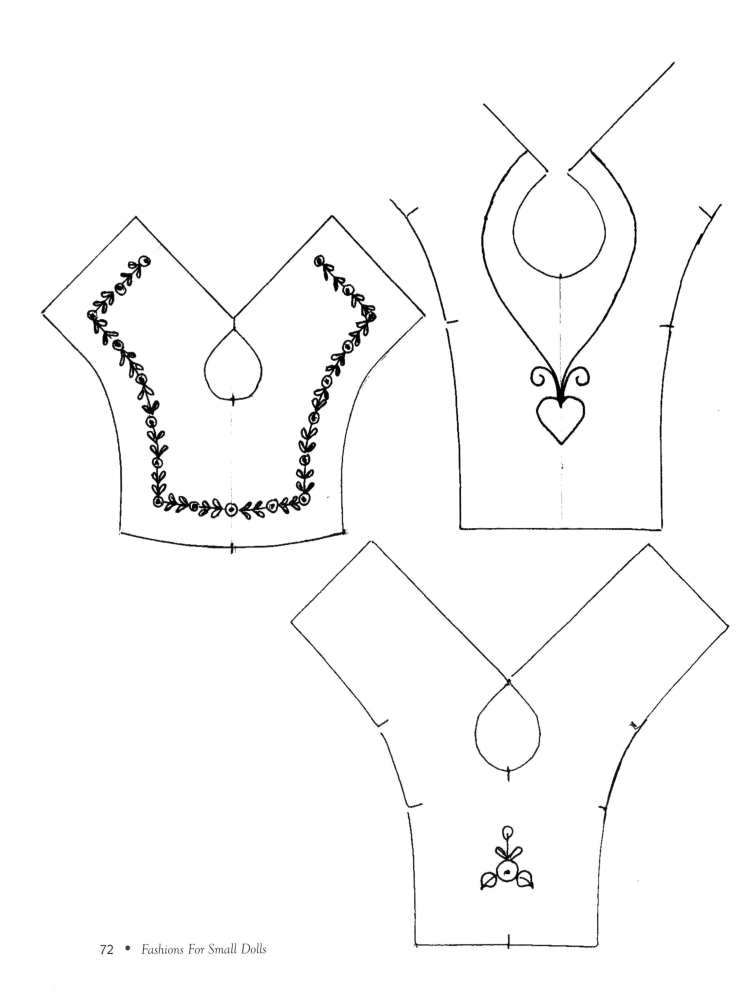

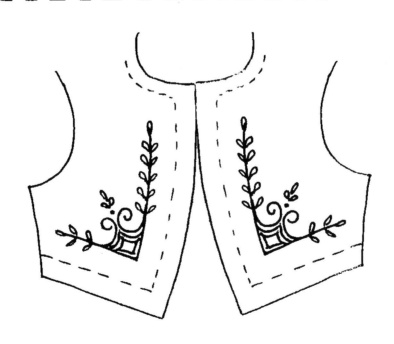

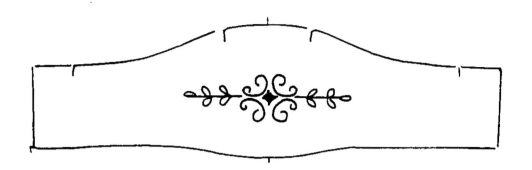

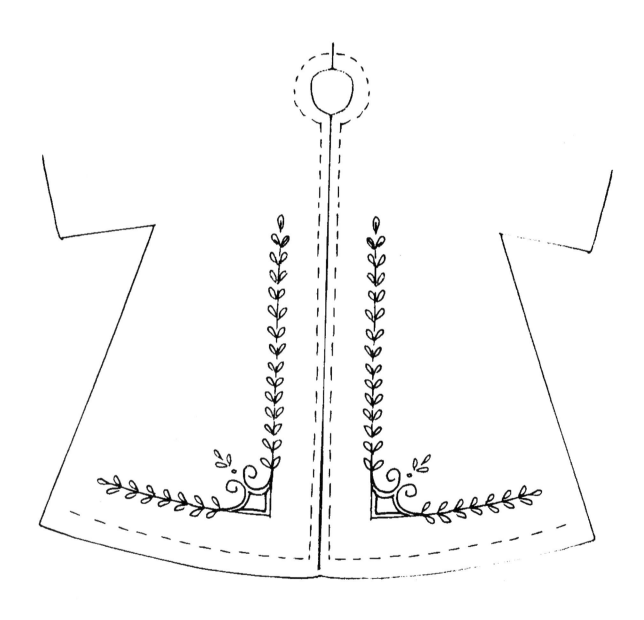

Fabric and Trim

NAME OF DOLL		Molly Cathy	Tulah	Ginny Ellie Paulinette	
Lace to control width of waistline (finished)	inches	4¼"	4¼"	5"	
	centimeters	11	11	12.5	
Underarm opening for sleeveless yoked dress	inches	1/2"	1/2"	5/8"	
	centimeters	1.25	1.25	1.5	
Lengthen bodice for dropped waistline	inches	3/8"	3/8"	1/2"	
	centimeters	1	1	1.25	
Lengthen sleeves for taller dolls	inches		3/16"		
	centimeters		.5		
Skirt width of petticoats (finished)	inches	12"	13"	13"	
	centimeters	30.5	33	33	
Skirt width of dresses (finished)	inches	12½"—13½"	14"—15"	15½"—16½"	
	centimeters	32—34	35.5—38	39—42	
Shoulder straps for petticoats (finished)	inches	1¾"	2"	2"	
	centimeters	4.5	5	5	
Bias binding for neck of blouse (finished)	inches	2¾"	2¾"	3¼"	
	centimeters	7	7	8	
Skirt length of petticoats (finished)	inches	2¼"	2¾"	2¾"	
	centimeters	5.75	7	7	

Measurement Chart

	Christina	Mary Anne Rose	Avery	Linda Peter Heidi	Lauren
	5"	5¼"	5¼"	6¼"	6¼"
	12.5	13	13	16	16
	5/8"	6/8"	6/8"	1"	1"
	1.5	1.8	1.8	3	2.5
	1/2"	1/2"	1/2"	5/8"	5/8"
	1.25	1.25	1.25	2	2
	1/2"		1/2"		1"
	1.25		1.25		2.5
	13½"	13½"	14"	16"	17"
	34.5	34.5	35.5	41	43
	18"—19"	18"—19"	18"—20"	19"—21"	20"—22"
	46—48	46—48	46—51	48—53	51—53
	2-1/8"	2¼"	2¼"	2½"	3"
	5.3	5.75	5.75	6	8
	3¼"	3½"	3½"	4"	4"
	8	9	9	10	10
	3"	3"	3-5/8"	3½"	4"
	7.75	7.75	9.25	9	10

General Sewing Tips

1. The sewing machine has to be fitted with the straight-stitch throat plate (the plate is specific for straight stitches) that has only a round little hole for the needle. Use a very fine needle like a 70/10. This makes it easier to sew fine materials and small pieces. There is so little to hold on to and when the needle takes part of the little garment down into the "underworld" of the machine, it can be a problem. All sewing by machine should be done with very small stitches to look neat and tidy. Imagine the size of the stitches in proportion to the size of the garment. This also makes it much easier to sew the small curves on the collar.

2. When using an over-lock machine to serge, the thread ends either have to be fastened in an alternate seam or, if they are at an opening like the inner leg seam of pants or sleeve edges, they need to be fastened with a big needle into the seam. Do not just cut off the thread ends.

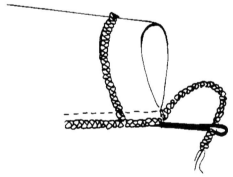

Finishing of over-edging threads at the end of a seam

3. There are normally two ways to insert Valenciennes lace. One method is to stitch the *entre deux* with a straight stitch onto the material, fasten it with a narrow zigzag stitch and carefully cut out the material behind. This leaves two very stiff lines that, even after pressing, often take on a life of their own on a small garment.

The other way is to over-edge the piece of fabric, sew the *entre deux* to the right side, press it so the seam allowance folds back and fasten it with a straight stitch very close to the edge. The same is done to the other side of the *entre deux*. This makes it fall softer, but in fine transparent material the seams may show through. Since an over-edged seam is about ¼ inch (.6 cm) wide, it might look bulky.

There is one more way to sew on Valenciennes lace which I find quite visually satisfactory, but it is not as strong as the other two and might not withstand as many launderings. Using an *entre deux* that is about 3/16 inch to ¼ inch (.5 cm to .6 cm) wider than it will later show on the finished garment, sew it onto the fabric in such a way that it is flush with the edge of the fabric. After pressing it, the edges are sewn down again as in the previous way. Now the visible seams are only 1/16 inch to 1/8 inch (.15 cm to .31 cm) wide and are not so obvious. If the fabric is tightly woven, these two rows of small stitches will be strong enough. I also like to attach the Valenciennes lace to the hems of panties in this way.

4. Always finish or at least press the hem of the skirt before gathering the top, because it is difficult to get this evenly done once it is attached to the bodice.

Buttons Knotted from Cord or Gimp

৶ ৫

I t is almost impossible to find interesting and decorative buttons in a size suitable for our small garments. Therefore, I often use a knotted button, which is easy to make from cord, gimp or soutache.

Button made from cord, gimp or soutache

Follow these instructions carefully and you will soon be able to do it. It takes a bit of practice to get all the loops even in the end, but a little pulling and pushing works wonders.

To fasten the two ends of the cord underneath the button:

1. Fasten a sewing thread close to the bottom of your button, wind the thread a few times around the cord and fasten.

2. Leaving the thread attached to the first cord end, go over to the other end of the cord and fasten it close to the first one.

3. Make sure you have enough stitches over it to prevent fraying.

4. Trim end pieces of cord and thread as close as possible to your stitching.

Dolls' Measurement Chart

NAME OF DOLL		Molly Cathy	Tulah	Ginny Ellie Paulinette	
Size	inches	7"	7"+	8"	
	centimeters	18	18+	20	
Neck Width	inches	2-3/8"	2-3/8"	2¾"	
	centimeters	6	6	7	
Chest Width	inches	4"	4-1/8"	4¼"	
	centimeters	10	10.5	11	
Arm Length	inches	2¾"	3-1/8"	3	
	centimeters	7	8	7.5	
Dress Length	inches	3¾"	4¼"	4-1/8"	
	centimeters	9.5	11	10.5	

	Christina	Mary Anne Rose	Avery	Linda Peter Heidi	Lauren
	8"+	9"	9"+	10"	10"+
	20+	23	23+	25	25+
	2-5/8"	2¾"	2¾"	3-1/8"	3-1/8"
	6.75	7	7	8	8
	4½"	4-7/8"	4-7/8"	5¾"	5¾"
	11.5	12	12	14.75	15
	3½"	3-3/8"	4¼"	3¾"	4¾"
	9	9	11	9.5	12
	5½"	4¾"	5½"	5½"	6¼"
	14	12	14	14	16

A — Neckline

B — Chest Width

C — Arm Length

D — Dress Length

Patterns

ℰℴ ℭℛ

Dresses

One of the most irritating things about dressing small dolls is that their little fingers very often get caught in the threads of the over-edging or in the hems of the sleeves. This happens when the stitching is not fine enough. One could be tempted to omit the over-edging in the sleeves!

Since these small dresses are awkward to handle under a sewing machine, you will have to be very careful not to stretch the waistlines when attaching the skirt. It is advisable to sew a narrow ribbon of the required length into the waist seam to keep it in shape.

Another practical way to reinforce the waist width is to insert an *entre deux* lace between the bodice and the skirt. If you do this, be sure to shorten the bodice pattern by the width of the *entre deux* in this case.

1. With right sides facing each other, place the bodice and lining together.
2. Most machines have a tendency to transport the two layers of fabric differently, so it is best to start sewing the center back from the side where the grain of the two fabric layers is straight.
3. Continue around the neckline and down the other side. Note: If there is to be a collar, it should be made beforehand and then placed between the top material and the lining before sewing the neckline of the bodice.
4. To give the center back of the bodice extra strength, do not trim the seam allowance.
5. The corners do need to be cut and neckline clipped.
6. Turn and press.

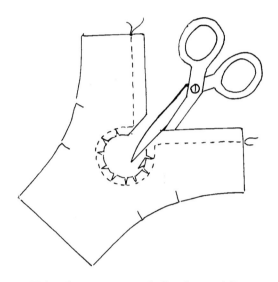

Trim the corners and clip the neckline

7. Gather the top of the sleeves with two rows of machine stitching.
8. Attach these to the bodice so all the gathers are between the two marks (on the pattern) in front and back of the shoulder point. If the material is very soft, it can be done with the top material and lining together.
9. The seam is then over-edged and pressed towards the center. Note: Another way to do this is to attach the sleeves only to the material, fold the lining over and hand-stitch to the seam.
10. Finish the sleeve hems. They can be bound with a bias band, or a pleat can be sewn in and the hem folded and pressed.
11. Press the hem at this stage, because it is difficult to double fold the hem after the side seam and the sleeve have been closed.
12. After closing and over-edging the side seam, hand sew the sleeve hem. If the sleeve is being bound with a bias band, the seam

allowance of the side seam needs to be trimmed carefully so it will not show after the sleeve is finished. Unfortunately, the seam allowance of 3/16 inch (.5 cm) is a little too big for such small outfits.

13. Attach the skirt to the waist line and over-edge.

14. Close the center back of the skirt and press.

15. Carefully stitch the seam allowances of the waist seam at the center back to the lining so that these are not visible on the outside.

16. A button and thread loop opposite the button will ensure that these seams are hidden from view.

17. Hand-stitch the hem.

18. Press the entire garment.

TIP: To prevent the doll's fingers from getting caught when trying on the garment, try putting the doll's hands in socks. Wrapping them with a bit of material also works.

Dresses with Shorter Bodices and Short Sleeves

A dress with a shorter bodice and short sleeves poses a bit of a challenge when creating one for small dolls, because the space from under the arm to the waistline is small. If the bodice is too short, the seam allowance hinders the movement of the arms. Therefore, we gather the sleeves into a bias binding and attach these to the waistline with the bindings overlapping. This way we create a sort of underarm space of about 3/8 inch (1 cm). It is practical to connect the bodice to the skirt with an *entre deux*, as this will prevent the waistline from being stretched out of proportion. A ribbon threaded through the *entre deux* adds an extra decoration as seen on the blue dress that Ginny models above and on Rose's green and white striped dress on page 47.

Yoked Sundresses or Jumpers

The underarm opening of the skirt can be done in two ways. If the dress is made of a thin transparent fabric and has a petticoat, it is easiest to do as follows:

1. Place the lining with the left side onto the right side of the dress fabric.
2. Sew with the smallest stitching between the markings for the underarm opening.
3. Clip where needed and turn the lining to the inside. (An alternative method: If the material does not need to be lined, clip the markings for the underarm openings and carefully fold the little pieces to the inside. Stitch the seam by hand.)
4. Press flat.

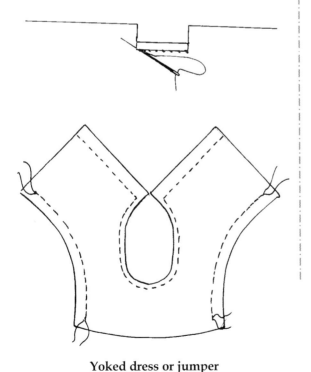

Yoked dress or jumper

5. The yoke for the dress is doubled with the lining (see directions for the bodice of the dress).
6. At the armhole side, the sewing should start and end above the seam allowance where the skirt is later attached.
7. Trim and turn the yoke around.
8. Press.
9. Fold and press the hem of the skirt; it is easier to do this before the top of it is gathered.
10. Run two rows of gathering stitches at the top of skirt from the center of the back to the first opening. Do not cut the thread, but continue over the front part to the next opening and through to the other back center.
11. The second row of stitching should be placed in such a way that it runs just along the edge of the openings for the arms.
12. Sew the skirt to the top material of the yoke.
13. Fold in and fasten the lining by hand to conceal the seam.
14. Close the skirt's center-back seam about 1½ inches (4 cm) to 2 inches (5 cm).
15. Press and slip stitch the hem.

Sleeveless Dresses and Jumpers

There is a special way to sew the top of a sleeveless dress or jumper.

1. Put together the dress fabric and lining, with right sides facing each other.
2. Join them by machine, starting at the waistline at the center back, up around the neckline and down the other side.
3. Sew the arm curves.
4. Trim and clip the neckline and arm curves.

5.   Turn all this around by pushing the two back parts through the width of the shoulder into the front part of the bodice.

6.   Press these seams flat. Make sure that fabric and lining are properly aligned and, if necessary, trim one or the other so that they are identical at the side seams.

7.   Open it in such a way that you can join the side seam.

8.   Sew the dress fabric, with right sides together, from the waistline up to the underarm point and then sew down to the waistline of the lining. (The skirt is only attached to the dress fabric and the lining is stitched by hand over this seam.)

9.   Close the center back of the skirt.

This whole procedure also applies if the opening to the dress is in the front.

Blouses and Shirts

The blouse patterns are made in such a way that there is 3/8 inch (1 cm) in either the front or the back to make a small double-folded hem, leaving a firmer edge for attaching buttons and holding the thread loops.

In the shirts that open in the front, this extra width is sewn off and pressed into a box pleat in the back before the collar is attached.

1.   First sew on the collar.

2.   Then fold the little hem to get the front line relatively tidy.

For blouses, either create a box pleat on the front or gather the width and bind around the neckline with a bias band.

On the blouse for Cathy, I sewed this extra width into tiny pin tucks. If you want to try this, follow these instructions.

1.   Carefully place these pin tucks so that the last one on the side ends in the binding, and also so that the width you sew off with the pin tucks equals the 3/8 inch (1 cm) that you have in the back.

2.   It is best to start by cutting a square piece of material that is the length of the blouse, but that has an extra ½ inch to 1 inch (1.25 cm to 2.5 cm) in the width.

3.   Cut open the center back to the neckline.

4.   Now sew in the pin tucks, the center of the pin tucks being 5/16 inch (.75 cm) apart for the smaller sizes and 3/8 inch (1 cm) apart for size 10.

5.   After you have pressed the pin tucks, fold the fabric in the middle.

6.   Place your pattern with the center front onto the fold between the pin tucks and cut out the neckline and sleeves.

7.   You now have excess material in the back center for the hem. You might want to trim this excess material if it is wider than needed for the hem.

Coats

A coat made over the basic pattern is done exactly like the dress. I prefer to leave the sleeves unlined as this makes it less bulky. However, lining the sleeves would eliminate the loathsome problem of the little fingers getting caught in the threads of the hems. (To prevent the doll's fingers from getting caught in stitching when trying on the garment, try putting the doll's hands in socks. Wrapping them with a bit of material also works.)

A coat made over the blouse pattern is very easy if you find a thin, soft material that

would not require lining.
1. Finish the edges of the sleeves.
2. Close the side seams.
3. Finish the raw edges of the coat. This can be done with a crocheted border or binding.

If the coat will be lined and trimmed with pearl braid, follow these instructions:
1. Put the pearl braid in the sleeve hem, if applicable.
2. With right sides facing each other, put the coat and lining fabrics together and join the sleeves, stitching into the line of stitches of the braid.
3. Sew around the neckline almost to the center front. Leave just the width of the seam allowance open.
4. Trim and clip the seam allowances on sleeves and neckline.
5. Turn and press.
6. Join the side seams by putting the right sides of the coat fabric on top of each other and sew, on the wrong side, from hem to underarm point to sleeve hem.
7. Leaving it under the machine with the needle down, turn the coat and continue to sew the lining together from sleeve hem to underarm point to coat hem.
8. Clip the underarm point.
9. Press seam allowances apart and turn the garment.
10. Attach the braid to the front of the coat and hemline, securing it into the seam at the neckline.
11. Turn the coat inside out, so that the right sides face each other.
12. Start stitching by machine on the sewing line of the trim, from the neck down the front, along the hemline and up the other front.
13. Trim seam allowances and corners.

14. To turn the coat right-side out, you have to open about 1½ inches (4 cm) of the seam at the hem or in the side seam of the lining. Turn the coat through this hole.
15. Press the coat and close the opening by hand.

Petticoats

I prefer the straps of a petticoat to be made by a bias tube of the same material, but for these small sizes it is certainly easier to use ribbon. Cut the shoulder straps according to the measurement given in the chart. I suggest you add a little in length, because these little "people" tend to be just a little different from each other. You may have to make the straps longer to give the bodice enough room under the arms.

How to make narrow bias tubing for ties or shoulder straps

1. Double the bodice of the petticoat and place the two parts with right sides facing each other.
2. Pin the shoulder straps at the back of the bodice on the markings, between the two layers of fabric.
3. Stitch the two layers together, along the top of the bodice. Start sewing from the center back and around to the marking for the straps in the front.
4. Skip a few stitches and continue sewing until you reach the marking for the other strap. Again skip a few stitches and sew to

the end of the line at center back.

5. Turn the bodice around and try it on for proper length of the straps. Pin them where they should be and close the two little openings, fastening the straps at the same time.

6. Decorate the skirt of the petticoat with lace, pin tucks and/or ribbons and finish the hemline.

7. Trim the skirt to the required length and run two rows of gathering stitches along the top.

8. Serge the back centers and attach the skirt to the outside part of the bodice.

9. Trim the corners, turn and press.

10. The inside can either be fastened by hand or carefully, by machine, from the right side, exactly in the joining seam between bodice and skirt.

11. Close the center-back seam about two-thirds up from the hemline.

12. Add a button and thread loop in the back for closing the petticoat.

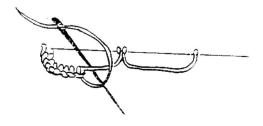

Thread loops

Panties

1. Sew and serge the front-center seam.
2. Attach lace to the leg hem.
3. Fold and press the seam allowance at the waist.

4. Sew in shirring elastic, making sure that it does not have gathers for the first ¼ inch (.6 cm). (Note: For these small sizes, use shirring elastic with three threads of elastic. Never use the type with only two elastic threads, because it has space for only one line of sewing, which will make it look untidy, plus it will not lay flat.)

5. Stretch it to the required length and stitch it to the required length. Stitch the first row between elastic one and two. The last ¼ inch (.6 cm) should be without gathers.

6. Stitch the second row.

7. Close the back-center seam and inner-leg seams. Serge and press.

Long Pants

The pattern for long pants is made over the basic pattern number 11 (the pattern for a knee-length pant). The pant legs are lengthened and the width of the ankle added. The ankle width needs to be wide enough for the doll's foot to go through. When lengthening, the extra width needs to be added evenly on both sides of the inner seam. The inner seams should make a right angle at the hem.

Circle Skirts

A pattern for a one-half circle or one-fourth circle skirt is done in the same basic way for all sizes.

All you need to do is find the curve that produces the waist width you need. Add a seam allowance to the top, and skirt length plus hem allowance to the bottom.

Pattern Numbers

ॐ ॐ

1. Basic Bodice, buttoned in the back

2. Basic Bodice, buttoned in front

3. Short Puffed Sleeve

4. Long Sleeve

5. Long Sleeve, with a box pleat at the wrist

6. Sleeve, without gathering, for shirts or jackets

7. Smaller Puffed Sleeve

8. Shirt or Blouse, with long sleeves to roll up on fold

9. Bodice, for petticoat, skirt or sundress

10. Panties

11. Long Underpants or Shorts

12. Cap Sleeve, for pinafore or dress

13. Bretelles, for skirt or sundress, fitted to petticoat bodice

14. Wing Sleeve, for summer dress, fitted to sides of basic bodice

15. Collar, for front opening

16. Peter Pan Collar

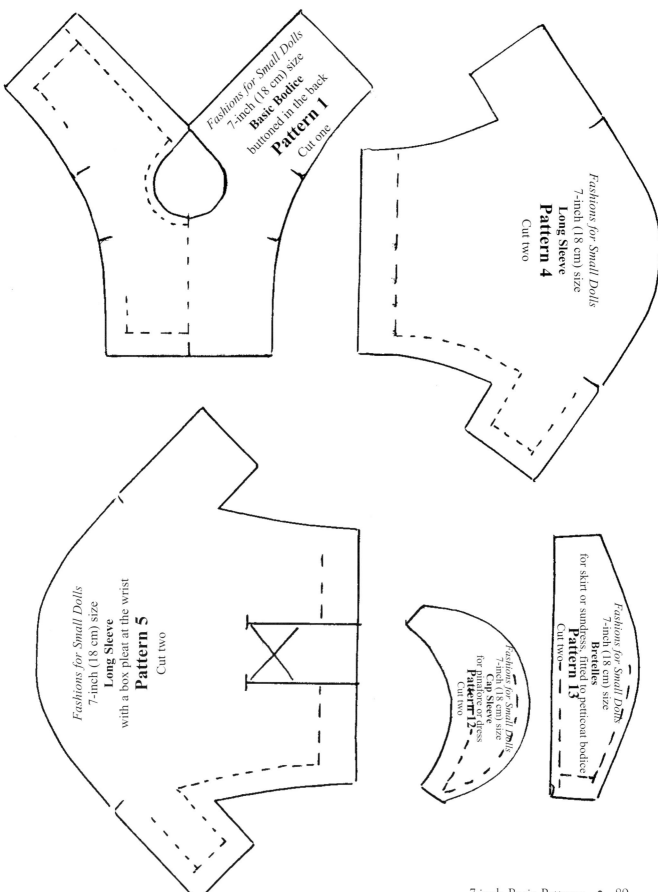

Fashions for Small Dolls
7-inch (18 cm) size
Basic Bodice
buttoned in the back
Pattern 1
Cut one

Fashions for Small Dolls
7-inch (18 cm) size
Long Sleeve
Pattern 4
Cut two

Fashions for Small Dolls
7-inch (18 cm) size
Long Sleeve
with a box pleat at the wrist
Pattern 5
Cut two

Fashions for Small Dolls
7-inch (18 cm) size
Bretelles
for skirt or sundress, fitted to petticoat bodice
Pattern 13
Cut two

Fashions for Small Dolls
7-inch (18 cm) size
Cap Sleeve
for pinafore or dress
Pattern 12
Cut two

7-inch Basic Patterns • 89

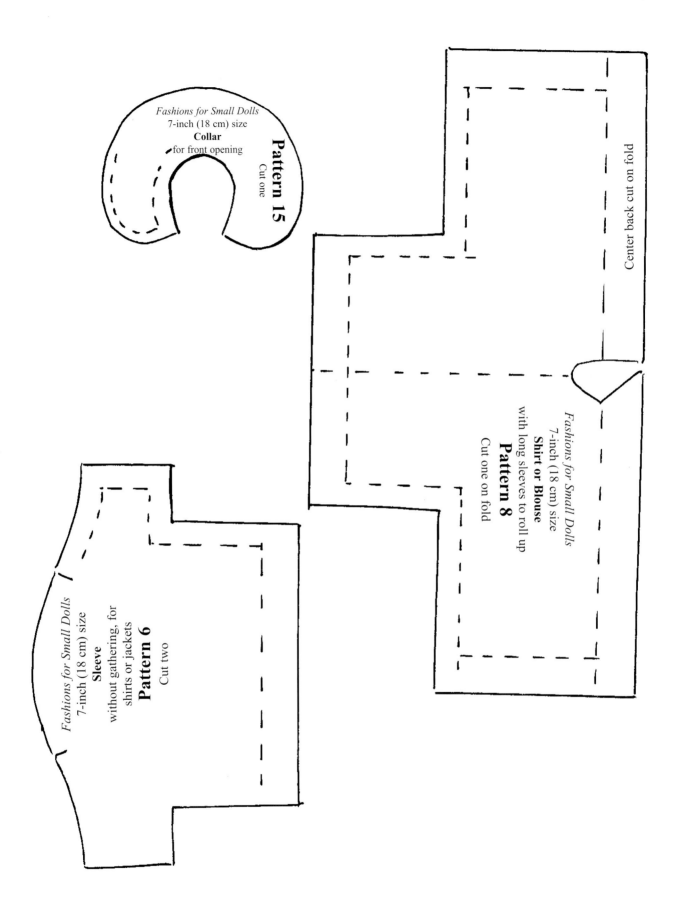

Fashions for Small Dolls
7-inch (18 cm) size
Collar
for front opening
Pattern 15
Cut one

Fashions for Small Dolls
7-inch (18 cm) size
Shirt or Blouse
with long sleeves to roll up
Pattern 8
Cut one on fold

Center back cut on fold

Fashions for Small Dolls
7-inch (18 cm) size
Sleeve
without gathering, for
shirts or jackets
Pattern 6
Cut two

90 • *Fashions For Small Dolls*

Fashions for Small Dolls
7-inch (18 cm) size
Bodice
for petticoat, skirt or sundress
Pattern 9
Cut one

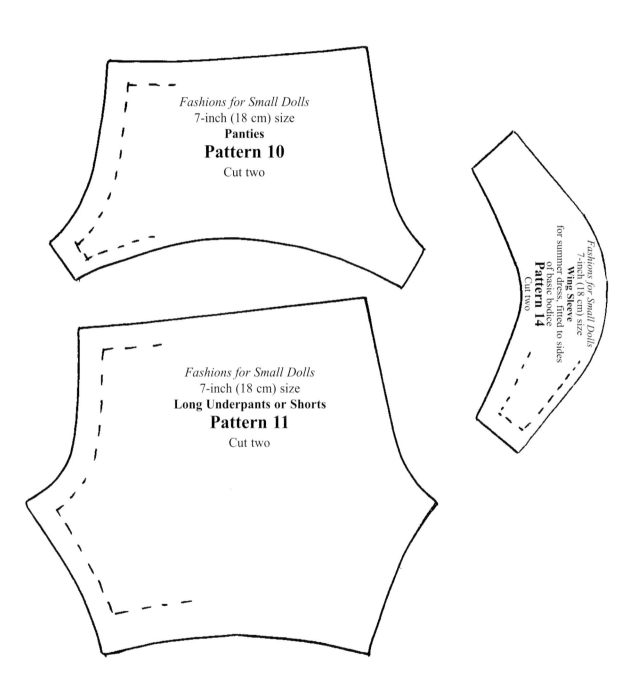

Fashions for Small Dolls
7-inch (18 cm) size
Panties
Pattern 10
Cut two

Fashions for Small Dolls
7-inch (18 cm) size
Long Underpants or Shorts
Pattern 11
Cut two

Fashions for Small Dolls
7-inch (18 cm) size
Wing Sleeve
for summer dress, fitted to sides
of basic bodice
Pattern 14
Cut two

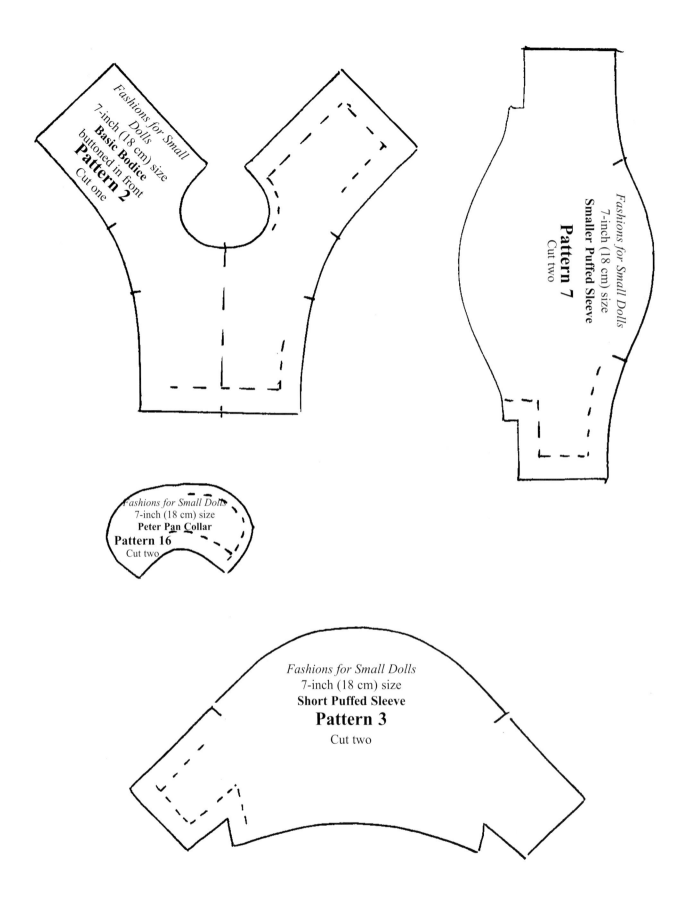

Fashions for Small Dolls
7-inch (18 cm) size
Basic Bodice
buttoned in front
Pattern 2
Cut one

Fashions for Small Dolls
7-inch (18 cm) size
Smaller Puffed Sleeve
Pattern 7
Cut two

Fashions for Small Dolls
7-inch (18 cm) size
Peter Pan Collar
Pattern 16
Cut two

Fashions for Small Dolls
7-inch (18 cm) size
Short Puffed Sleeve
Pattern 3
Cut two

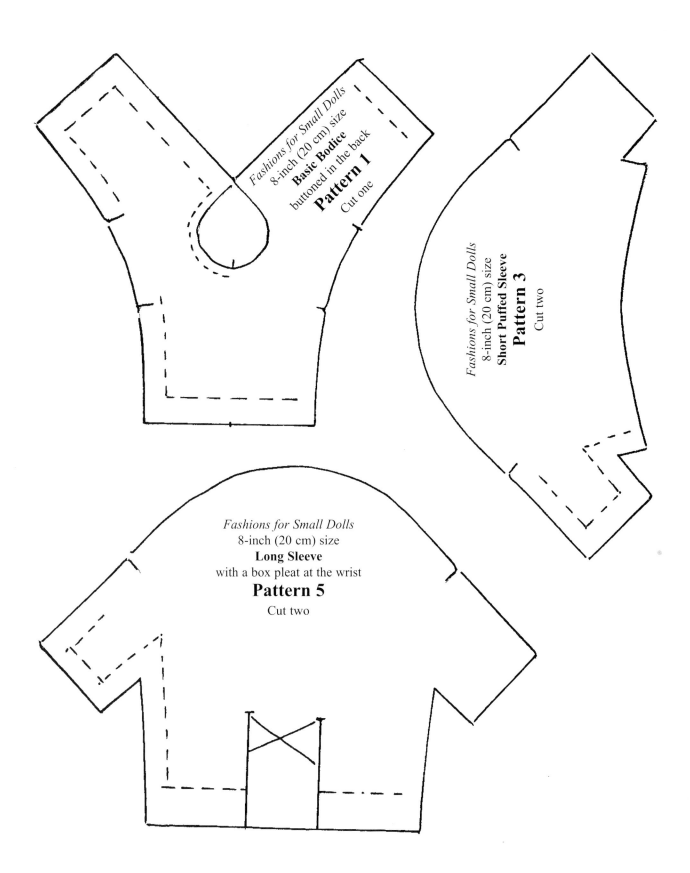

Fashions for Small Dolls
8-inch (20 cm) size
Basic Bodice
buttoned in the back
Pattern 1
Cut one

Fashions for Small Dolls
8-inch (20 cm) size
Short Puffed Sleeve
Pattern 3
Cut two

Fashions for Small Dolls
8-inch (20 cm) size
Long Sleeve
with a box pleat at the wrist
Pattern 5
Cut two

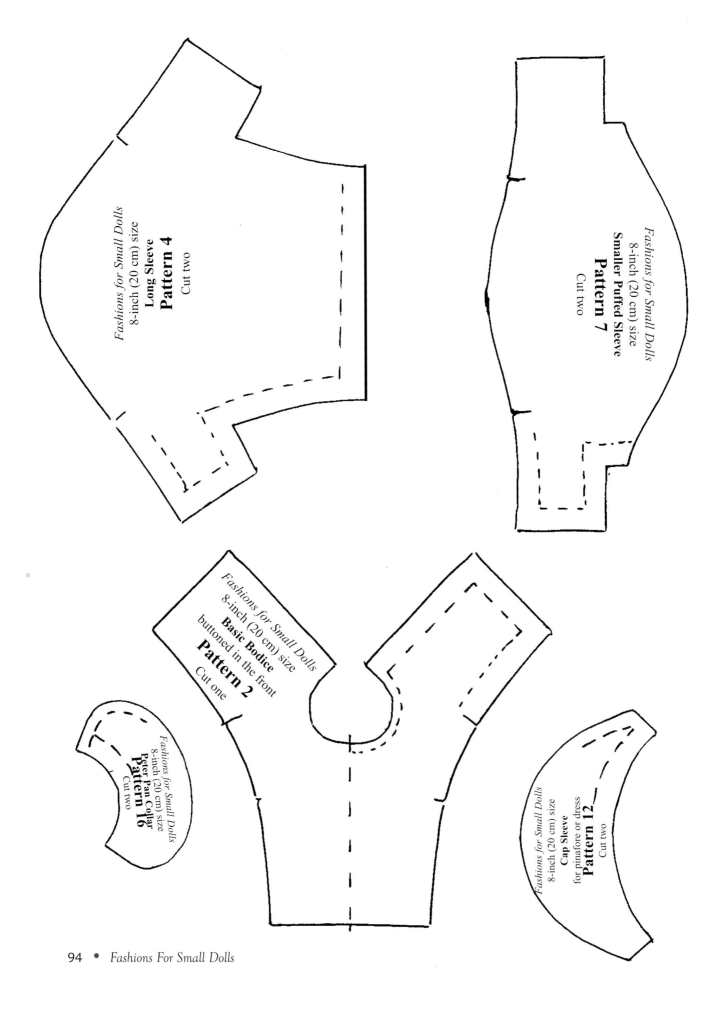

Fashions for Small Dolls
8-inch (20 cm) size
Long Sleeve
Pattern 4
Cut two

Fashions for Small Dolls
8-inch (20 cm) size
Smaller Puffed Sleeve
Pattern 7
Cut two

Fashions for Small Dolls
8-inch (20 cm) size
Basic Bodice
buttoned in the front
Pattern 2
Cut one

Fashions for Small Dolls
8-inch (20 cm) size
Peter Pan Collar
Pattern 16
Cut two

Fashions for Small Dolls
8-inch (20 cm) size
Cap Sleeve
for pinafore or dress
Pattern 12
Cut two

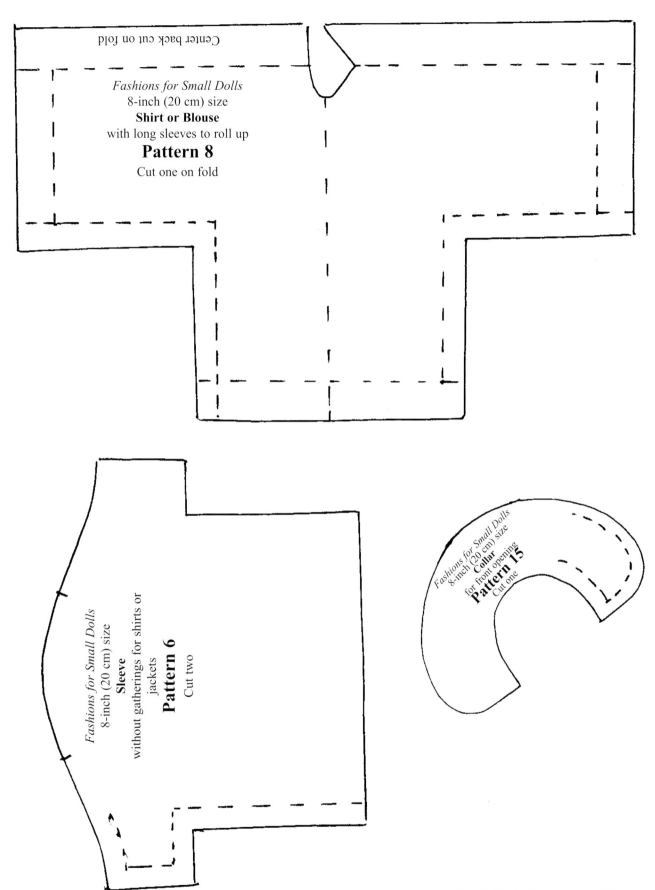

Center back cut on fold

Fashions for Small Dolls
8-inch (20 cm) size
Shirt or Blouse
with long sleeves to roll up
Pattern 8
Cut one on fold

Fashions for Small Dolls
8-inch (20 cm) size
Sleeve
without gatherings for shirts or jackets
Pattern 6
Cut two

Fashions for Small Dolls
8-inch (20 cm) size
Collar
for front opening
Pattern 15
Cut one

8-inch Basic Patterns • 95

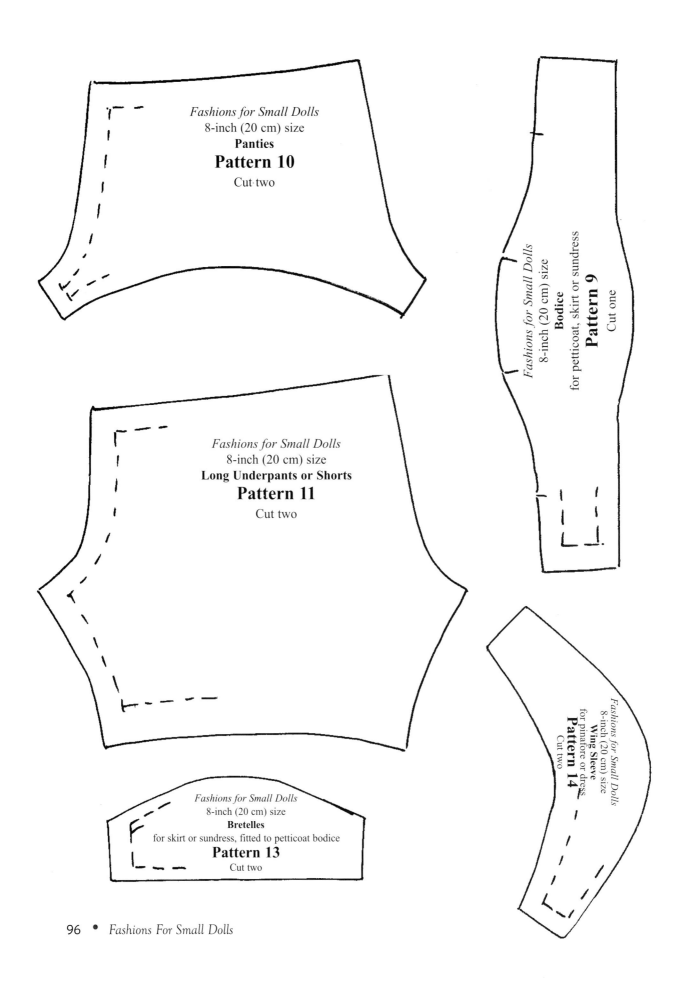

Fashions for Small Dolls
8-inch (20 cm) size
Panties
Pattern 10
Cut two

Fashions for Small Dolls
8-inch (20 cm) size
Bodice
for petticoat, skirt or sundress
Pattern 9
Cut one

Fashions for Small Dolls
8-inch (20 cm) size
Long Underpants or Shorts
Pattern 11
Cut two

Fashions for Small Dolls
8-inch (20 cm) size
Wing Sleeve
for pinafore or dress
Pattern 14
Cut two

Fashions for Small Dolls
8-inch (20 cm) size
Bretelles
for skirt or sundress, fitted to petticoat bodice
Pattern 13
Cut two

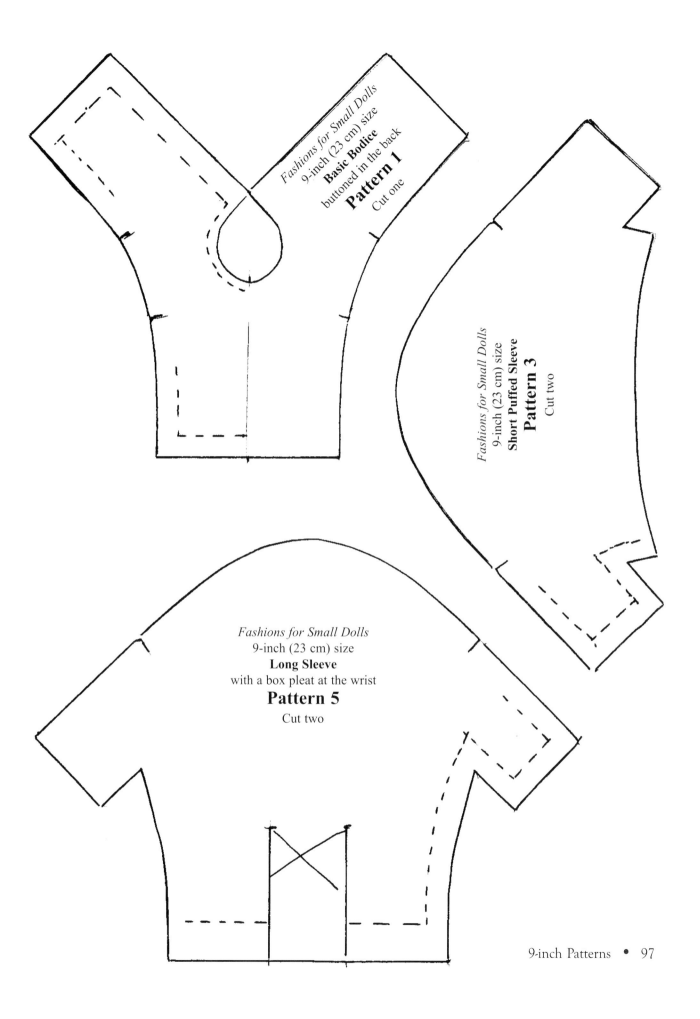

Fashions for Small Dolls
9-inch (23 cm) size
Basic Bodice
buttoned in the back
Pattern 1
Cut one

Fashions for Small Dolls
9-inch (23 cm) size
Short Puffed Sleeve
Pattern 3
Cut two

Fashions for Small Dolls
9-inch (23 cm) size
Long Sleeve
with a box pleat at the wrist
Pattern 5
Cut two

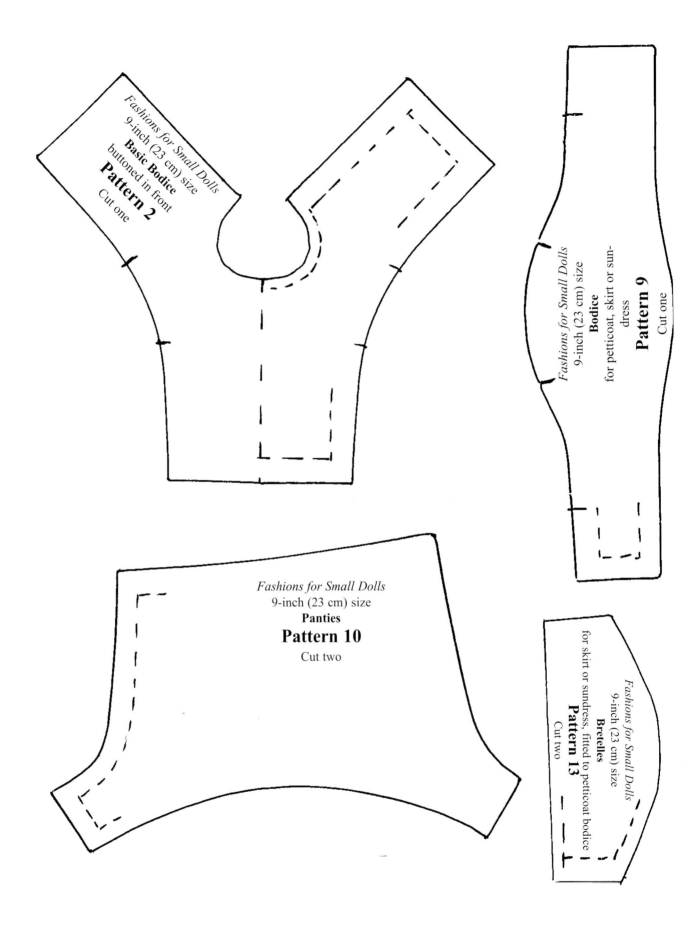

Fashions for Small Dolls
9-inch (23 cm) size
Basic Bodice
buttoned in front
Pattern 2
Cut one

Fashions for Small Dolls
9-inch (23 cm) size
Bodice
for petticoat, skirt or sundress
Pattern 9
Cut one

Fashions for Small Dolls
9-inch (23 cm) size
Panties
Pattern 10
Cut two

Fashions for Small Dolls
9-inch (23 cm) size
Bretelles
for skirt or sundress, fitted to petticoat bodice
Pattern 13
Cut two

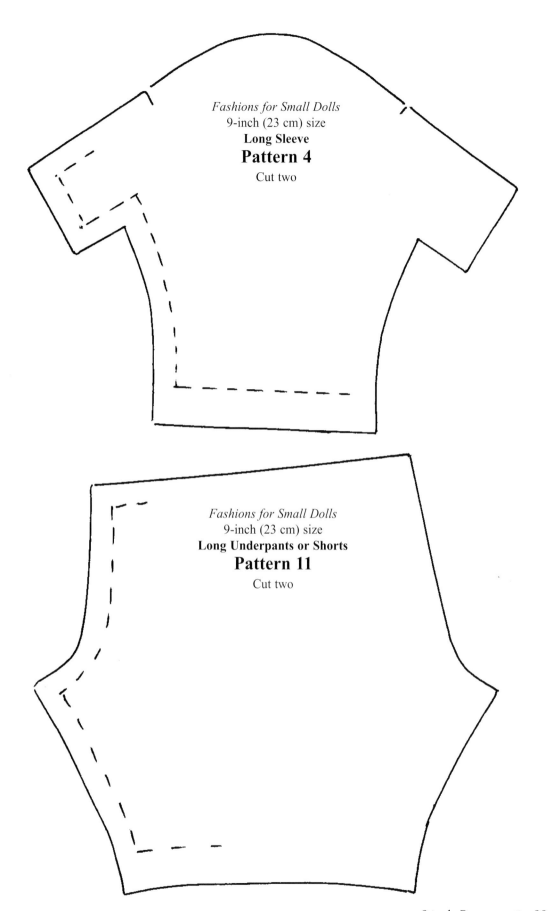

Fashions for Small Dolls
9-inch (23 cm) size
Long Sleeve
Pattern 4
Cut two

Fashions for Small Dolls
9-inch (23 cm) size
Long Underpants or Shorts
Pattern 11
Cut two

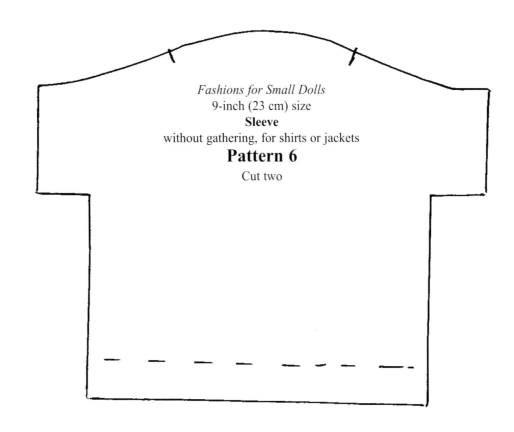

Fashions for Small Dolls
9-inch (23 cm) size
Sleeve
without gathering, for shirts or jackets
Pattern 6
Cut two

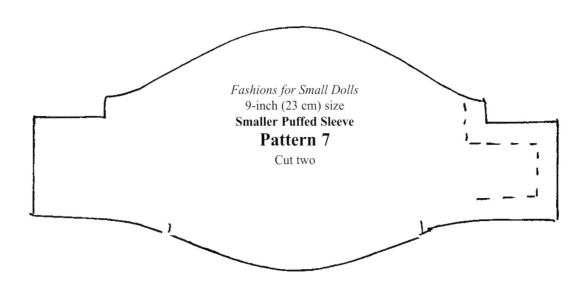

Fashions for Small Dolls
9-inch (23 cm) size
Smaller Puffed Sleeve
Pattern 7
Cut two

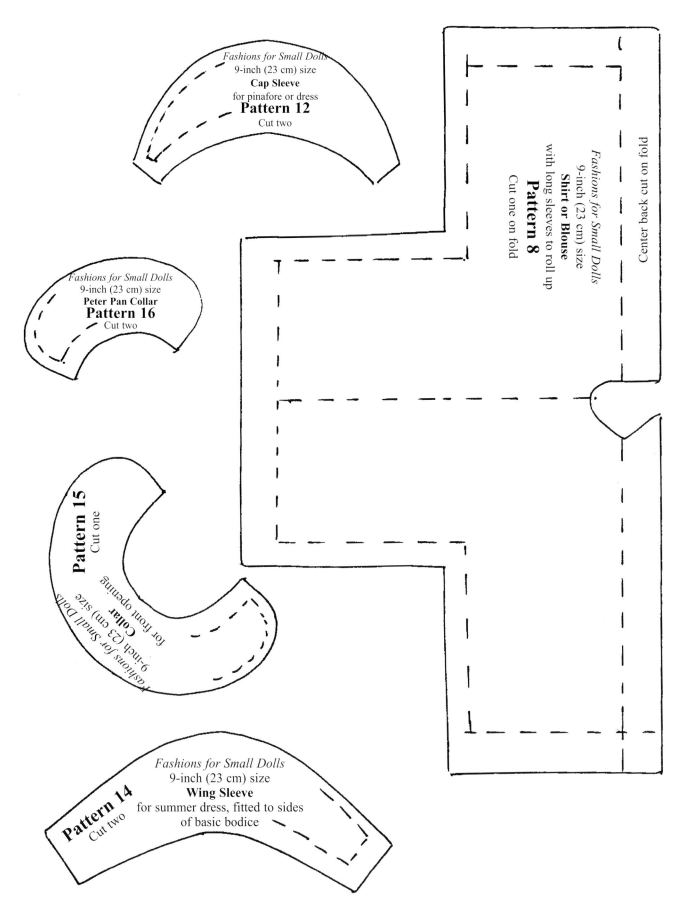

Fashions for Small Dolls
9-inch (23 cm) size
Cap Sleeve
for pinafore or dress
Pattern 12
Cut two

Fashions for Small Dolls
9-inch (23 cm) size
Peter Pan Collar
Pattern 16
Cut two

Pattern 15
Cut one

Fashions for Small Dolls
9-inch (23 cm) size
Collar
for front opening

Pattern 14
Cut two

Fashions for Small Dolls
9-inch (23 cm) size
Wing Sleeve
for summer dress, fitted to sides
of basic bodice

Fashions for Small Dolls
9-inch (23 cm) size
Shirt or Blouse
with long sleeves to roll up
Pattern 8
Cut one on fold

Center back cut on fold

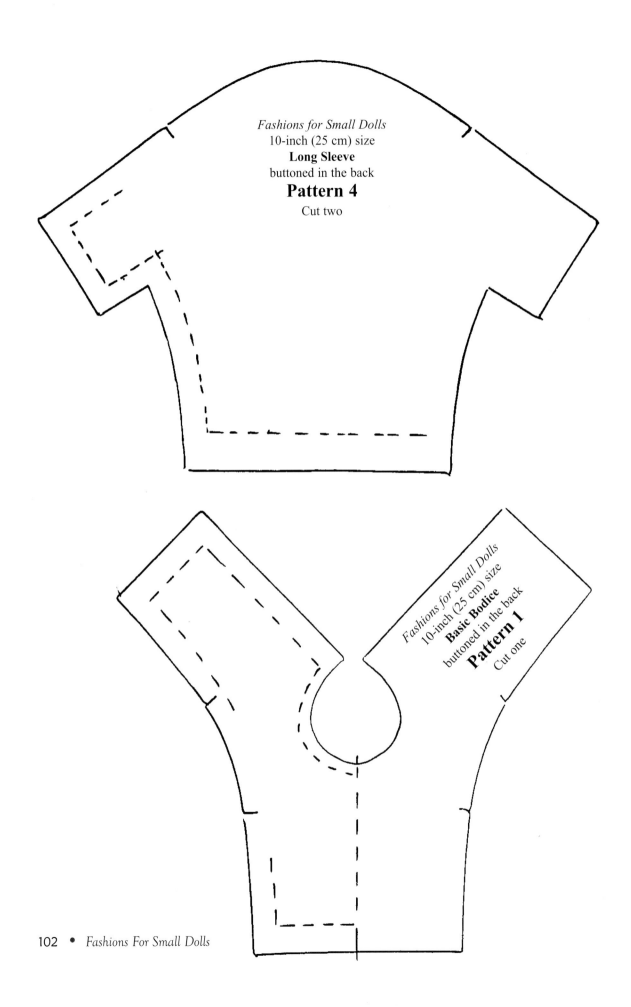

Fashions for Small Dolls
10-inch (25 cm) size
Long Sleeve
buttoned in the back
Pattern 4
Cut two

Fashions for Small Dolls
10-inch (25 cm) size
Basic Bodice
buttoned in the back
Pattern 1
Cut one

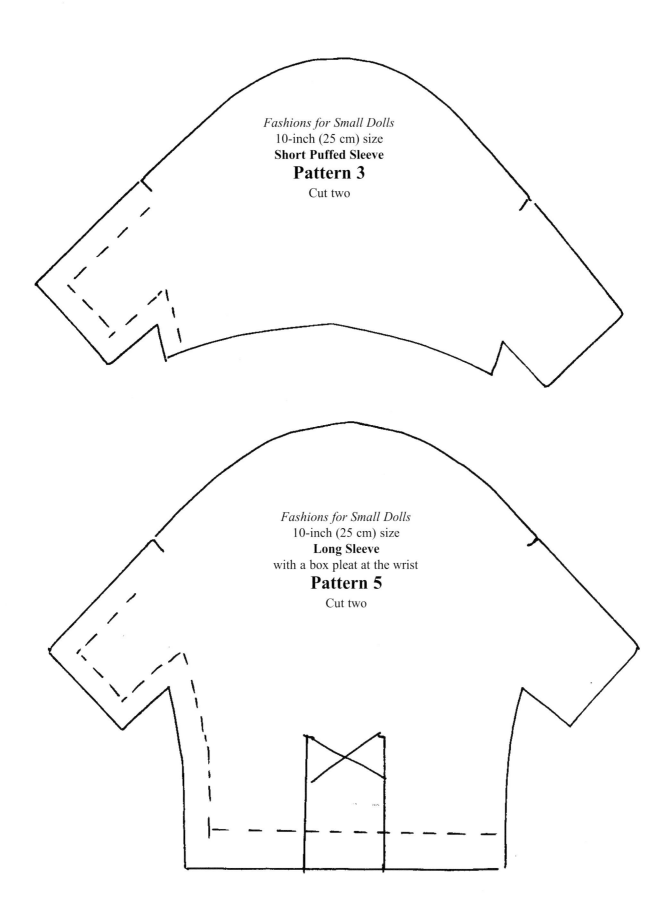

Fashions for Small Dolls
10-inch (25 cm) size
Short Puffed Sleeve
Pattern 3
Cut two

Fashions for Small Dolls
10-inch (25 cm) size
Long Sleeve
with a box pleat at the wrist
Pattern 5
Cut two

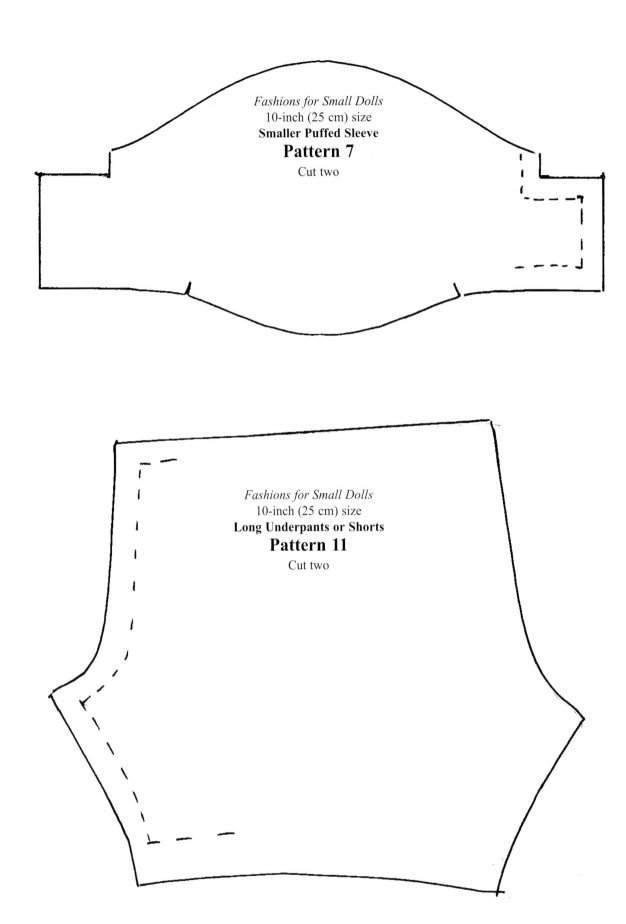

Fashions for Small Dolls
10-inch (25 cm) size
Smaller Puffed Sleeve
Pattern 7
Cut two

Fashions for Small Dolls
10-inch (25 cm) size
Long Underpants or Shorts
Pattern 11
Cut two

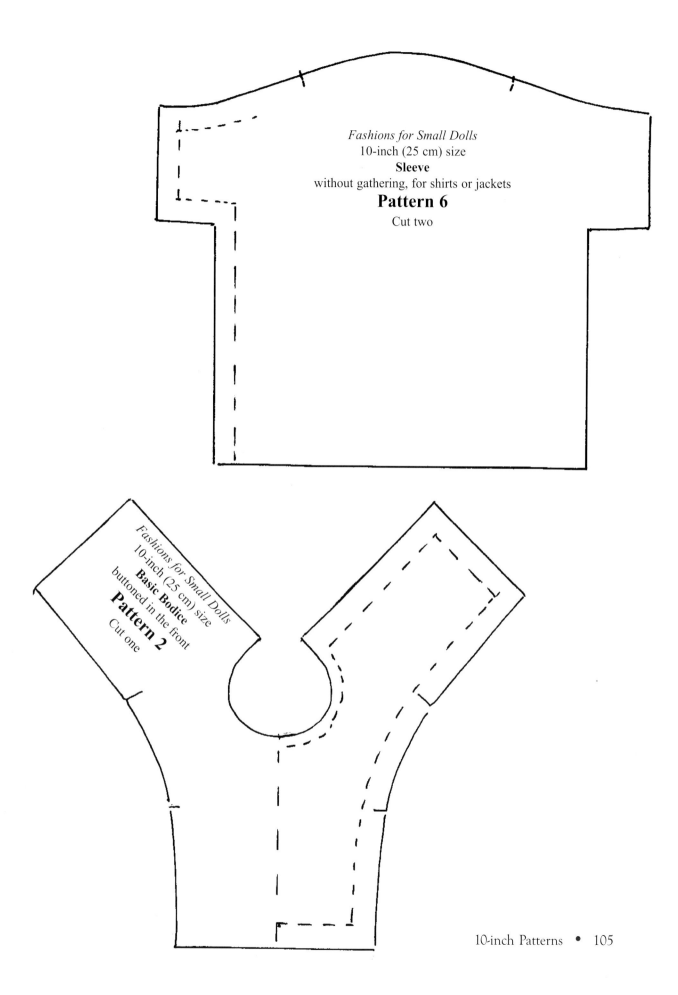

Fashions for Small Dolls
10-inch (25 cm) size
Sleeve
without gathering, for shirts or jackets
Pattern 6
Cut two

Fashions for Small Dolls
10-inch (25 cm) size
Basic Bodice
buttoned in the front
Pattern 2
Cut one

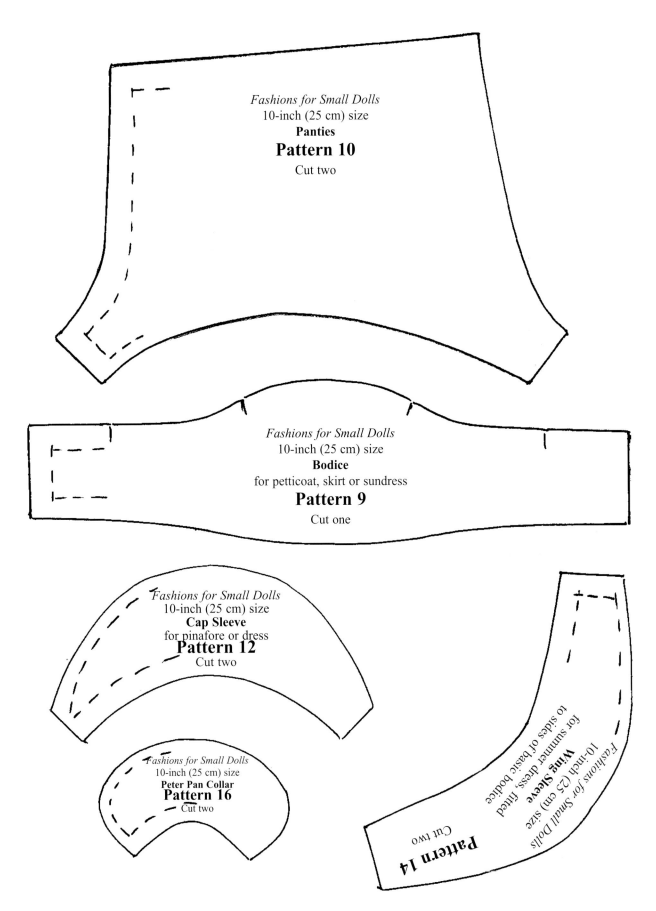

Fashions for Small Dolls
10-inch (25 cm) size
Panties
Pattern 10
Cut two

Fashions for Small Dolls
10-inch (25 cm) size
Bodice
for petticoat, skirt or sundress
Pattern 9
Cut one

Fashions for Small Dolls
10-inch (25 cm) size
Cap Sleeve
for pinafore or dress
Pattern 12
Cut two

Fashions for Small Dolls
10-inch (25 cm) size
Peter Pan Collar
Pattern 16
Cut two

Fashions for Small Dolls
10-inch (25 cm) size
Wing Sleeve
for summer dress, fitted
to sides of basic bodice
Pattern 14
Cut two

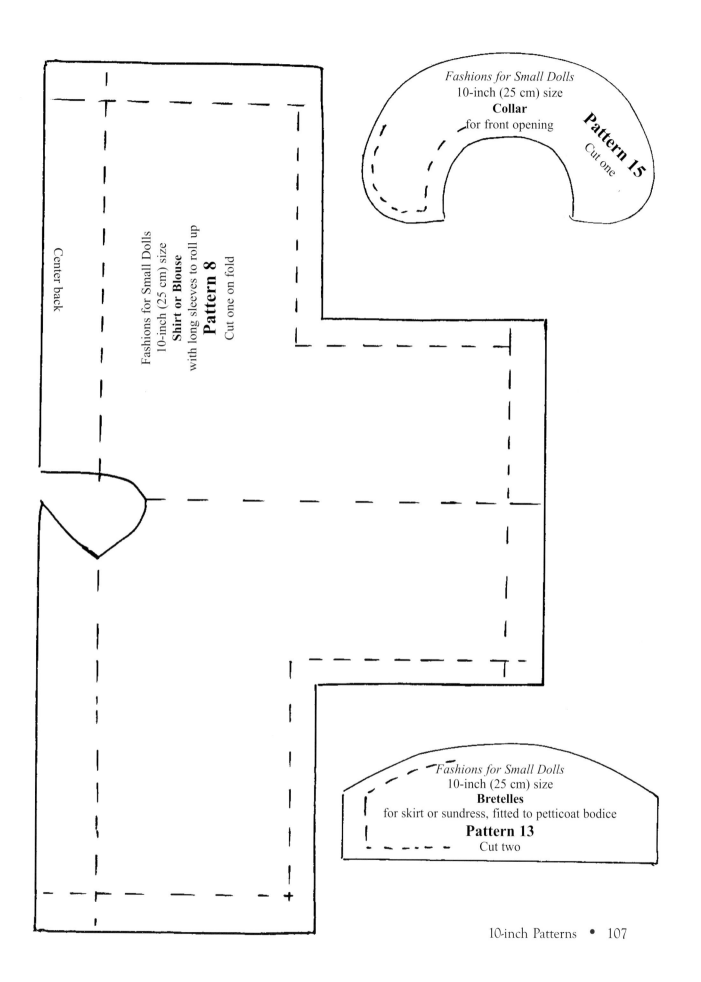

Fashions for Small Dolls
10-inch (25 cm) size
Collar
for front opening

Pattern 15
Cut one

Center back

Fashions for Small Dolls
10-inch (25 cm) size
Shirt or Blouse
with long sleeves to roll up
Pattern 8
Cut one on fold

Fashions for Small Dolls
10-inch (25 cm) size
Bretelles
for skirt or sundress, fitted to petticoat bodice
Pattern 13
Cut two

Basic Bodice for Taller and Slimmer Dolls

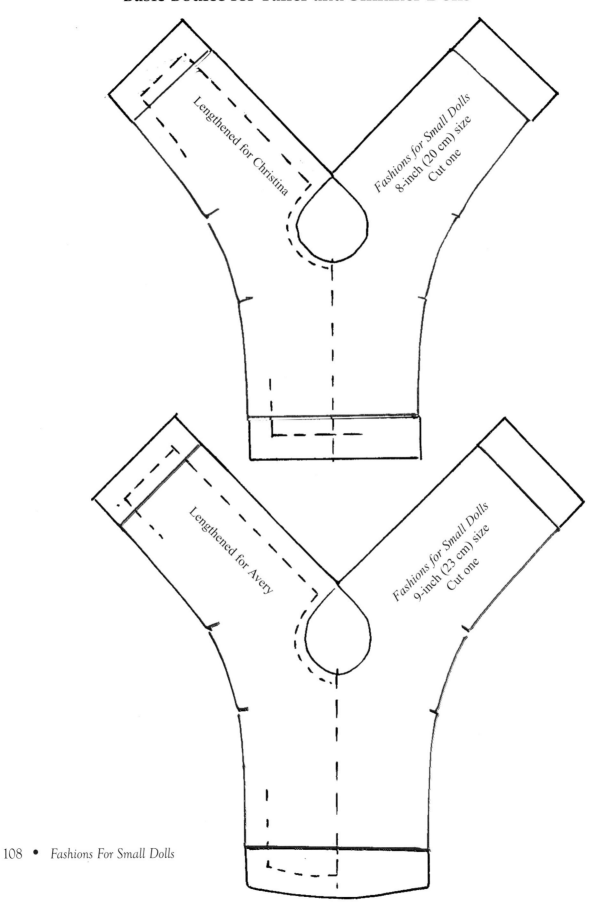

Lengthened for Christina

Fashions for Small Dolls
8-inch (20 cm) size
Cut one

Lengthened for Avery

Fashions for Small Dolls
9-inch (23 cm) size
Cut one

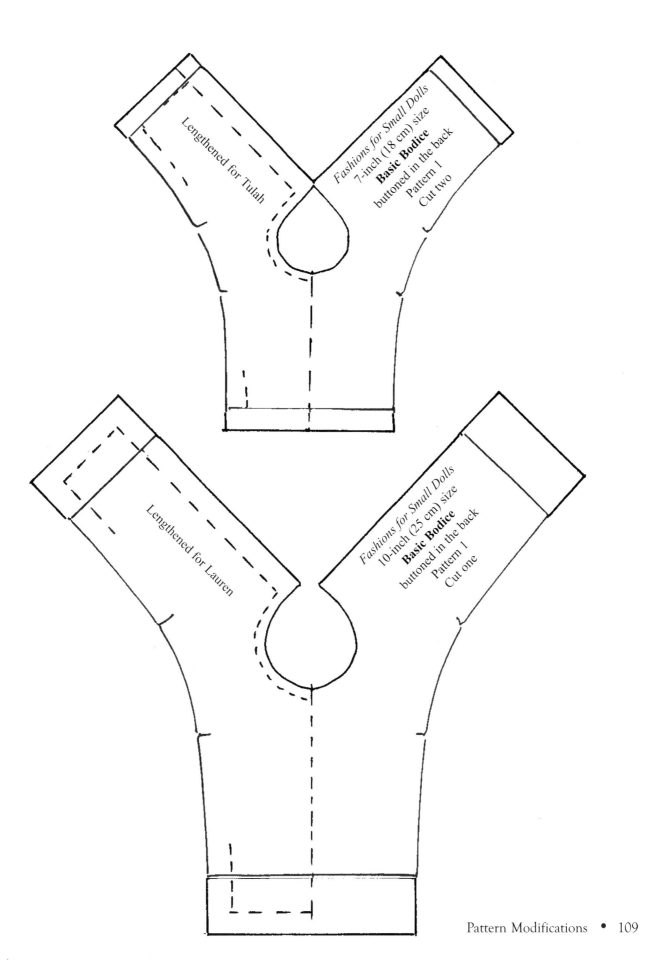

Lengthened for Tulah

Fashions for Small Dolls
7-inch (18 cm) size
Basic Bodice
buttoned in the back
Pattern 1
Cut two

Lengthened for Lauren

Fashions for Small Dolls
10-inch (25 cm) size
Basic Bodice
buttoned in the back
Pattern 1
Cut one

Petticoat Bodice for Tulah, Christina, Avery and Lauren

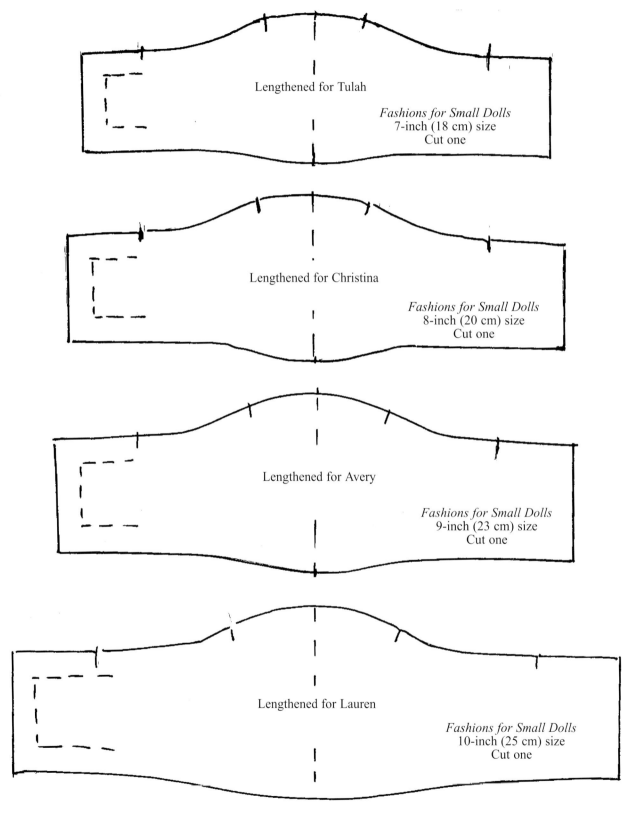

Lengthened for Tulah

Fashions for Small Dolls
7-inch (18 cm) size
Cut one

Lengthened for Christina

Fashions for Small Dolls
8-inch (20 cm) size
Cut one

Lengthened for Avery

Fashions for Small Dolls
9-inch (23 cm) size
Cut one

Lengthened for Lauren

Fashions for Small Dolls
10-inch (25 cm) size
Cut one

Basic Dress with a Shorter Bodice and Short Sleeves

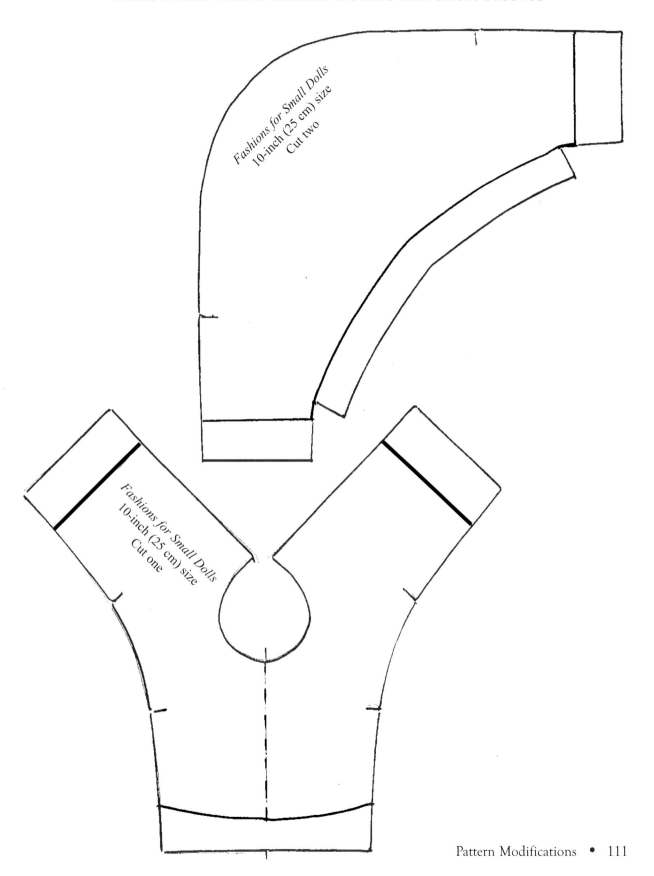

Fashions for Small Dolls
10-inch (25 cm) size
Cut two

Fashions for Small Dolls
10-inch (25 cm) size
Cut one

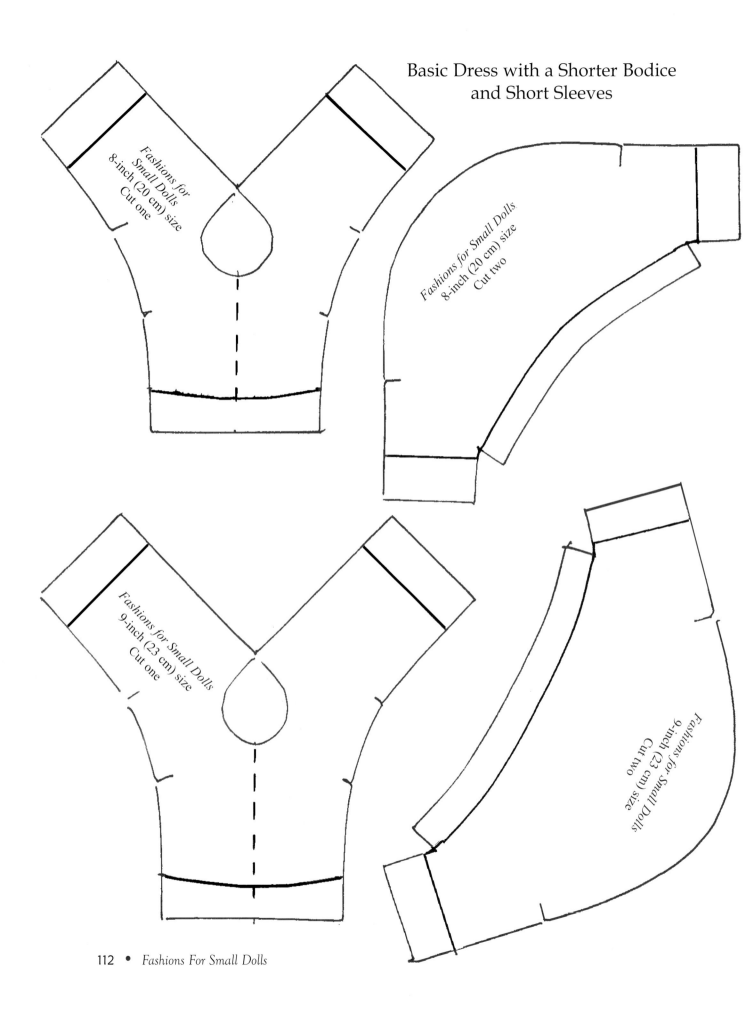

Basic Dress with a Shorter Bodice
and Short Sleeves

Fashions for
Small Dolls
8-inch (20 cm) size
Cut one

Fashions for Small Dolls
8-inch (20 cm) size
Cut two

Fashions for Small Dolls
9-inch (23 cm) size
Cut one

Fashions for Small Dolls
9-inch (23 cm) size
Cut two

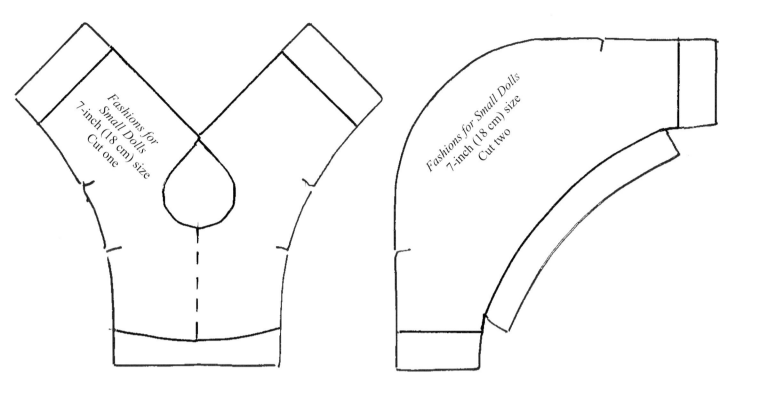

Fashions for Small Dolls
7-inch (18 cm) size
Cut one

Fashions for Small Dolls
7-inch (18 cm) size
Cut two

Basic Dress with Dropped Waistline

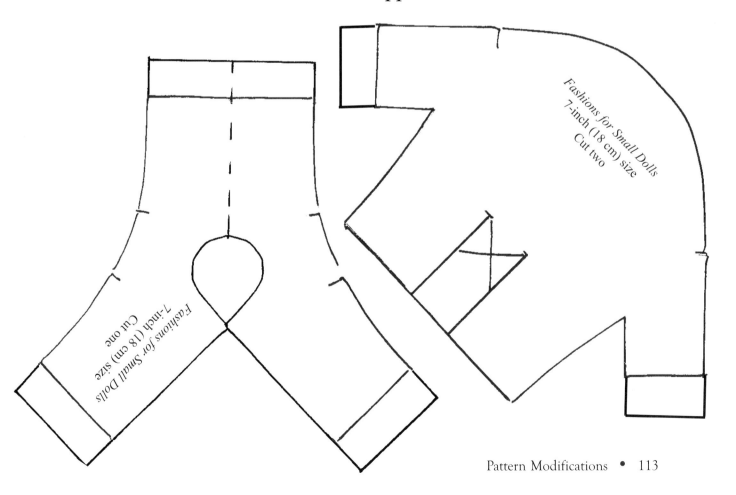

Fashions for Small Dolls
7-inch (18 cm) size
Cut one

Fashions for Small Dolls
7-inch (18 cm) size
Cut two

Basic Dress with Dropped Waistline

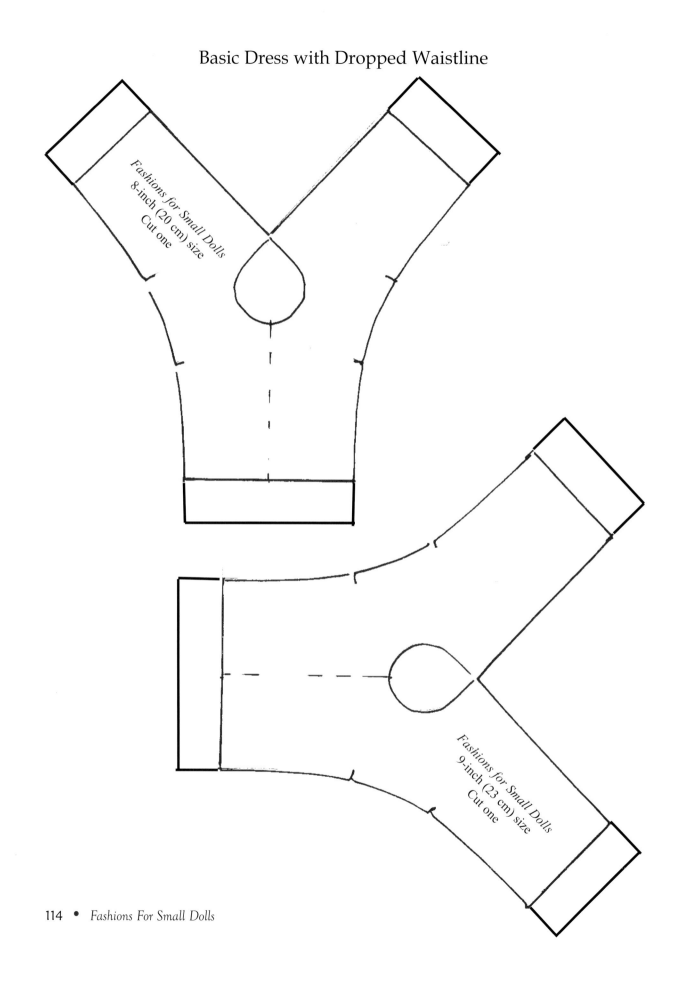

Fashions for Small Dolls
8-inch (20 cm) size
Cut one

Fashions for Small Dolls
9-inch (23 cm) size
Cut one

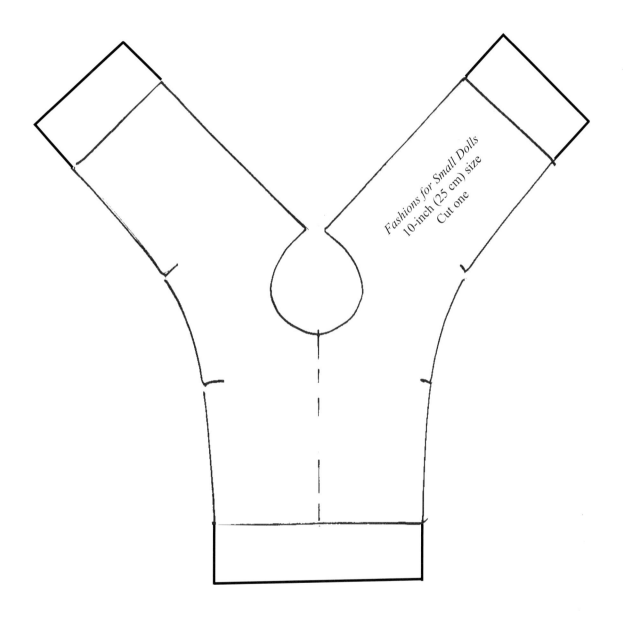

Fashions for Small Dolls
10-inch (25 cm) size
Cut one

Smocked Dress Constructed Over
Patterns 1 and 7

See page 57 for smocking diagrams

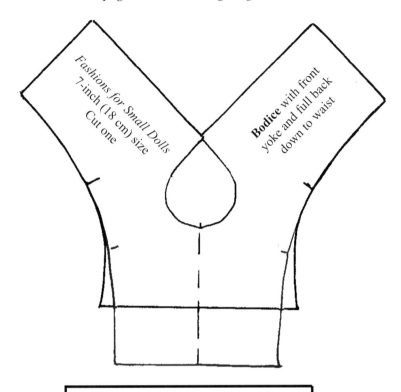

Fashions for Small Dolls
7-inch (18 cm) size
Cut one

Bodice with front yoke and full back down to waist

Fashions for Small Dolls
7-inch (18 cm) size
Skirt Front
for smocked dress
Cut one on fold

Center Front

½ inch (1 cm)

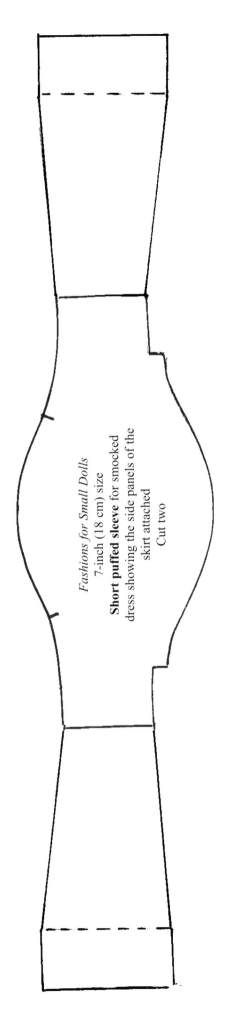

Fashions for Small Dolls
7-inch (18 cm) size
Short puffed sleeve for smocked dress showing the side panels of the skirt attached
Cut two

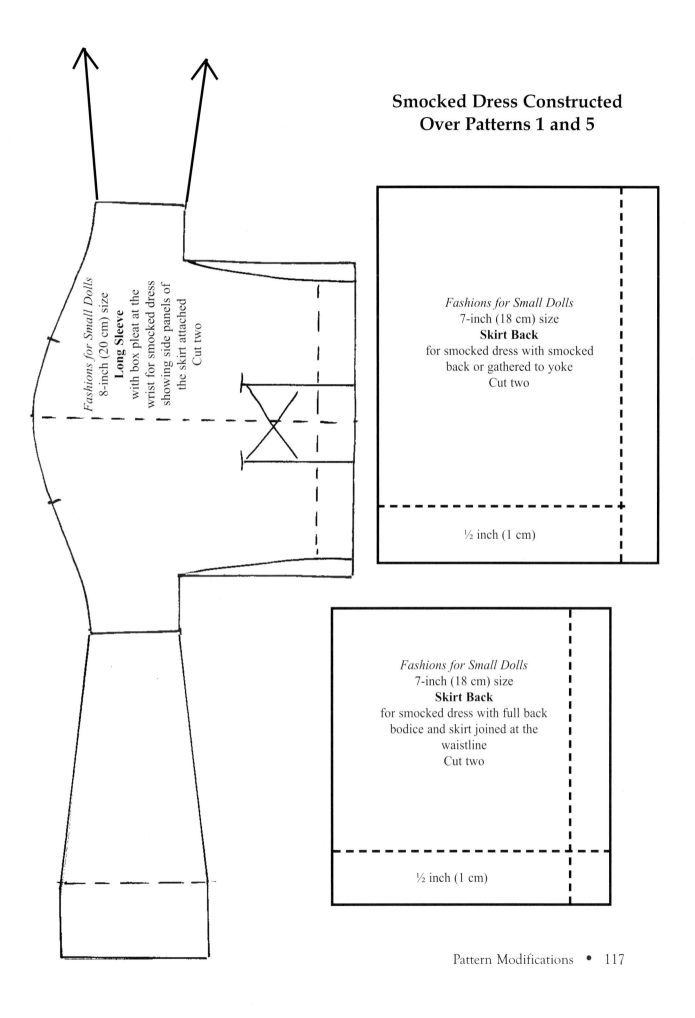

Smocked Dress Constructed Over Patterns 1 and 5

Fashions for Small Dolls
8-inch (20 cm) size
Long Sleeve
with box pleat at the wrist for smocked dress showing side panels of the skirt attached
Cut two

Fashions for Small Dolls
7-inch (18 cm) size
Skirt Back
for smocked dress with smocked back or gathered to yoke
Cut two

½ inch (1 cm)

Fashions for Small Dolls
7-inch (18 cm) size
Skirt Back
for smocked dress with full back bodice and skirt joined at the waistline
Cut two

½ inch (1 cm)

Smocked Dress Constructed Over Patterns 1 and 5

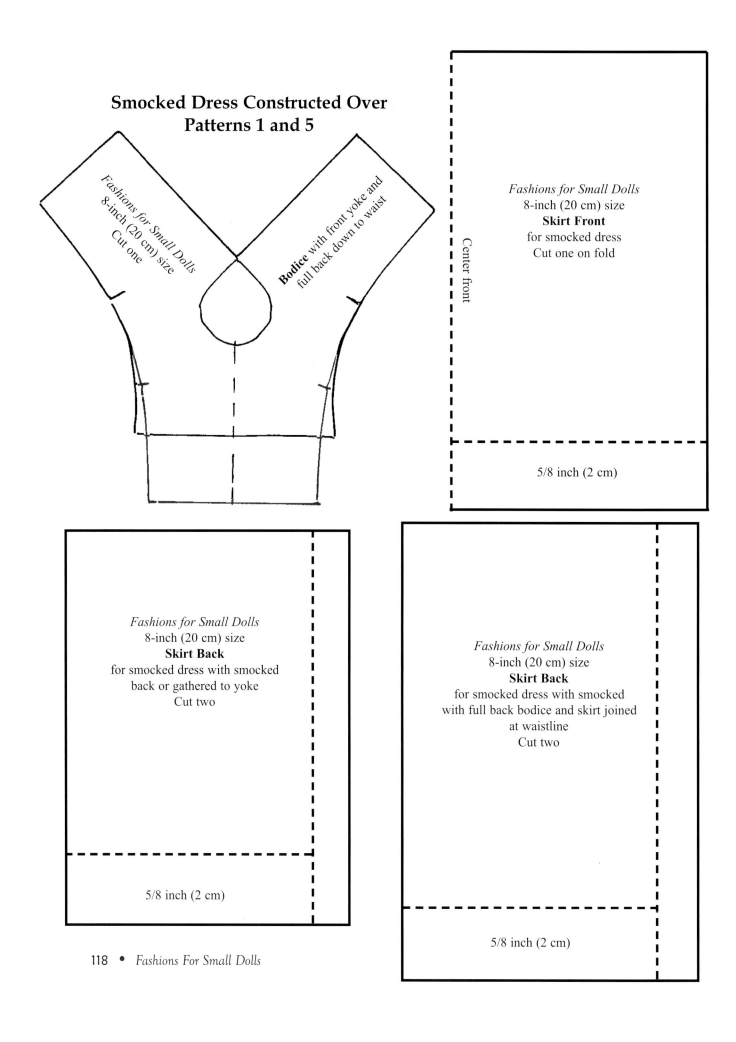

Fashions for Small Dolls
8-inch (20 cm) size
Cut one

Bodice with front yoke and full back down to waist

Fashions for Small Dolls
8-inch (20 cm) size
Skirt Front
for smocked dress
Cut one on fold

Center front

5/8 inch (2 cm)

Fashions for Small Dolls
8-inch (20 cm) size
Skirt Back
for smocked dress with smocked
back or gathered to yoke
Cut two

5/8 inch (2 cm)

Fashions for Small Dolls
8-inch (20 cm) size
Skirt Back
for smocked dress with smocked
with full back bodice and skirt joined
at waistline
Cut two

5/8 inch (2 cm)

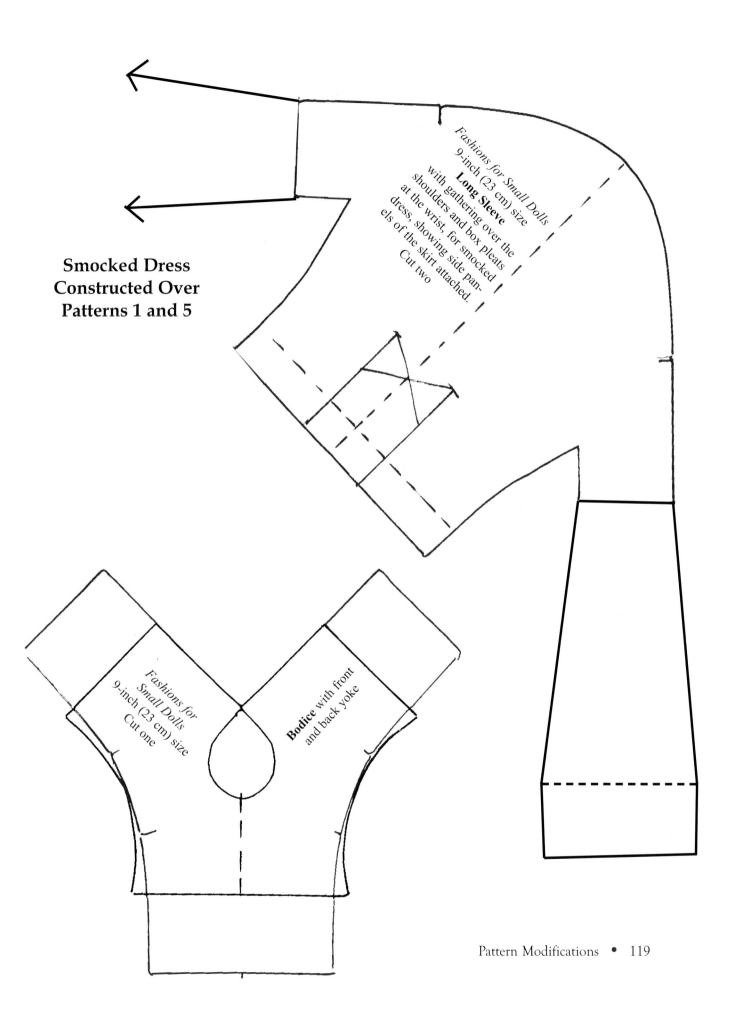

Smocked Dress Constructed Over Patterns 1 and 5

Fashions for Small Dolls 9-inch (23 cm) size **Long Sleeve** with gathering over the shoulders and box pleats at the wrist, for smocked dress, showing side panels of the skirt attached. Cut two

Fashions for Small Dolls 9-inch (23 cm) size Cut one

Bodice with front and back yoke

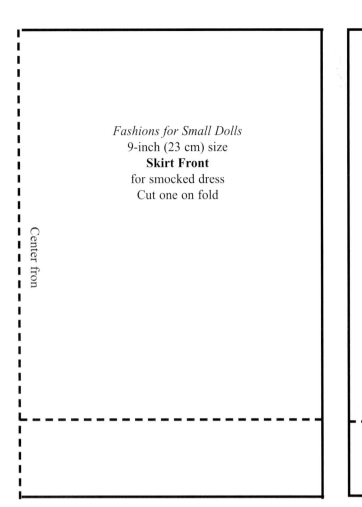

Fashions for Small Dolls
9-inch (23 cm) size
Skirt Front
for smocked dress
Cut one on fold

Center fron

Fashions for Small Dolls
9-inch (23 cm) size
Skirt Back
for smocked dress with smocked back or
gathered to yoke
Cut two

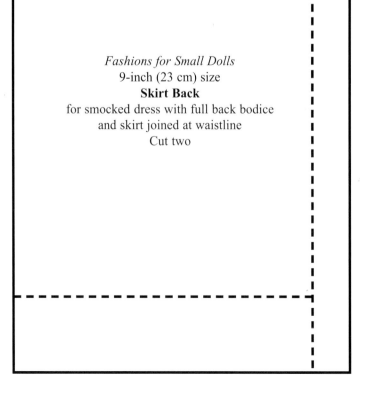

Fashions for Small Dolls
9-inch (23 cm) size
Skirt Back
for smocked dress with full back bodice
and skirt joined at waistline
Cut two

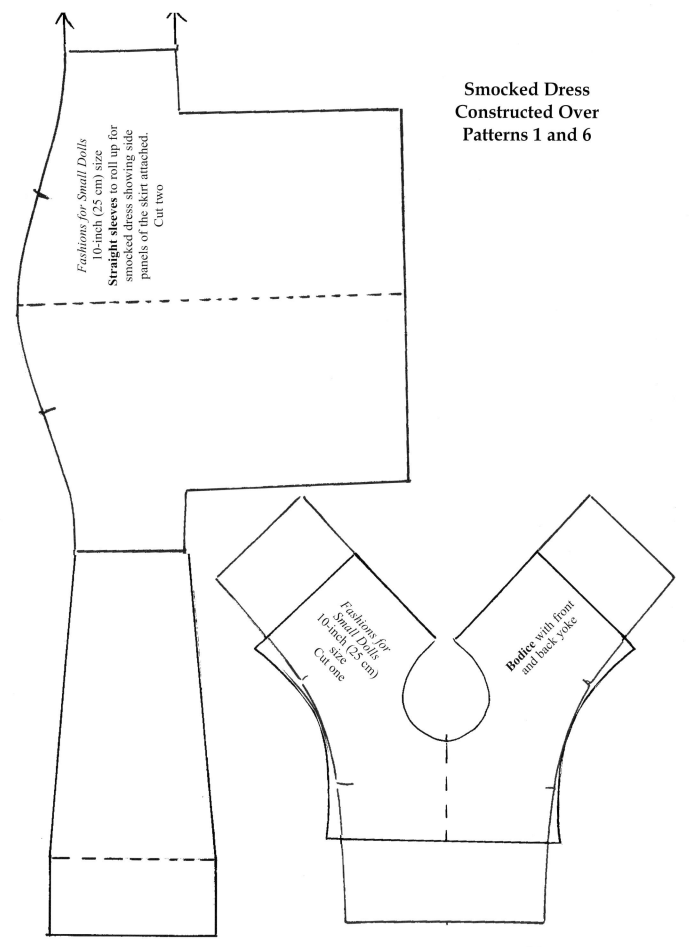

**Smocked Dress
Constructed Over
Patterns 1 and 6**

Fashions for Small Dolls
10-inch (25 cm) size
Straight sleeves to roll up for
smocked dress showing side
panels of the skirt attached.
Cut two

*Fashions for
Small Dolls*
10-inch (25 cm)
size
Cut one

Bodice with front
and back yoke

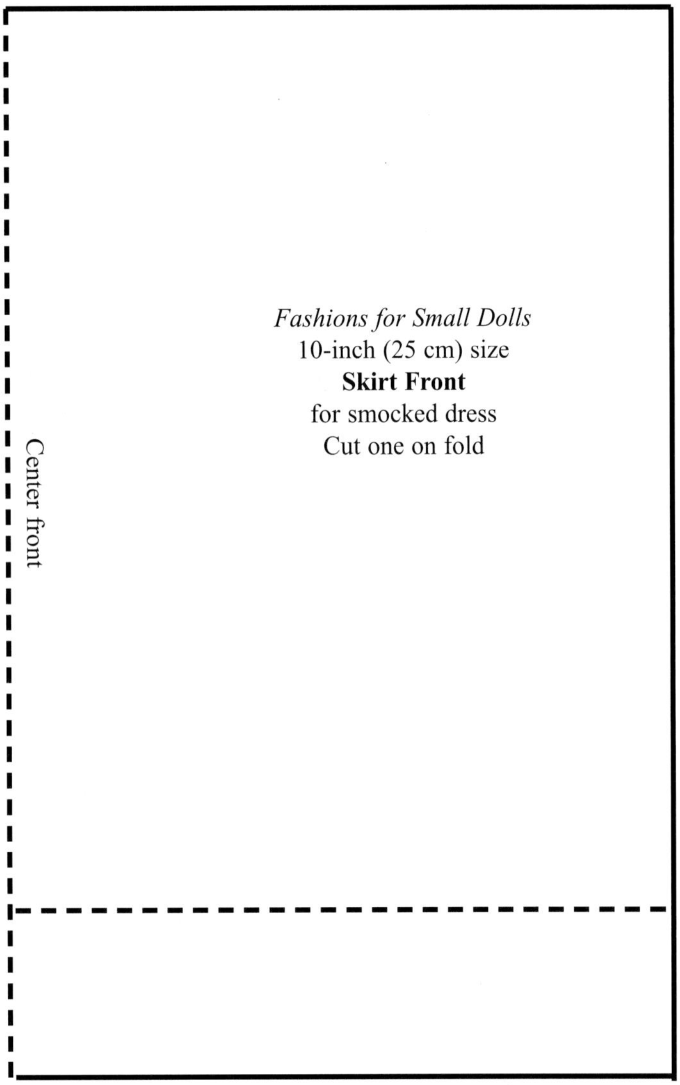

Center front

Fashions for Small Dolls
10-inch (25 cm) size
Skirt Front
for smocked dress
Cut one on fold

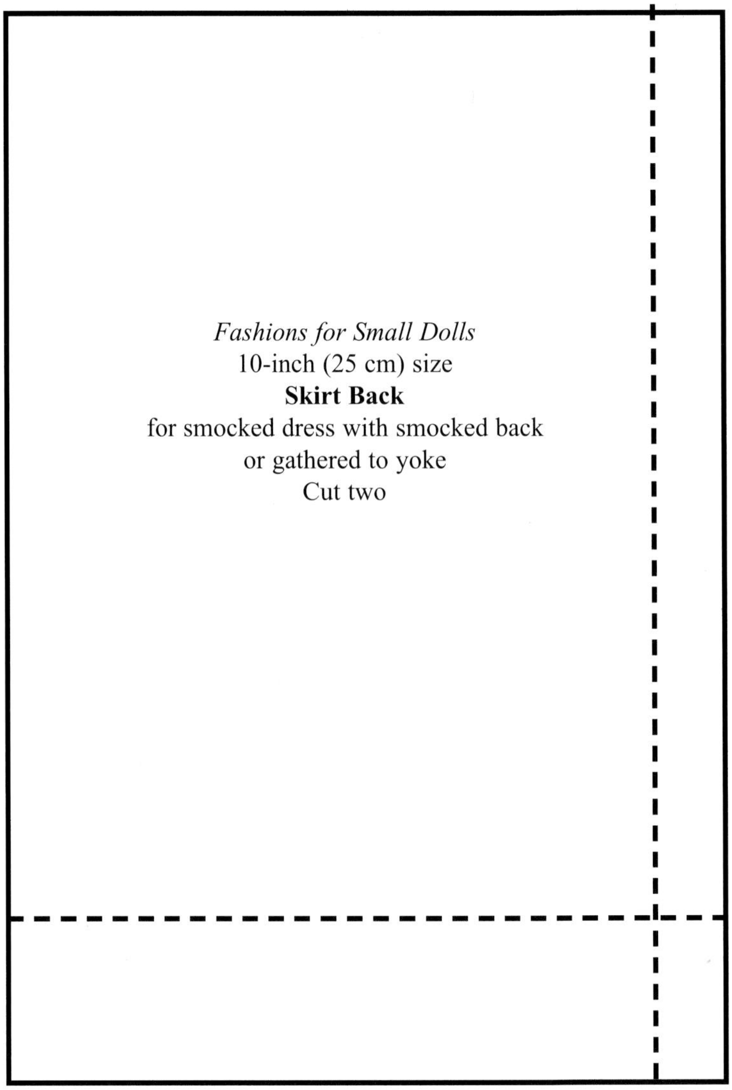

Fashions for Small Dolls
10-inch (25 cm) size
Skirt Back
for smocked dress with smocked back
or gathered to yoke
Cut two

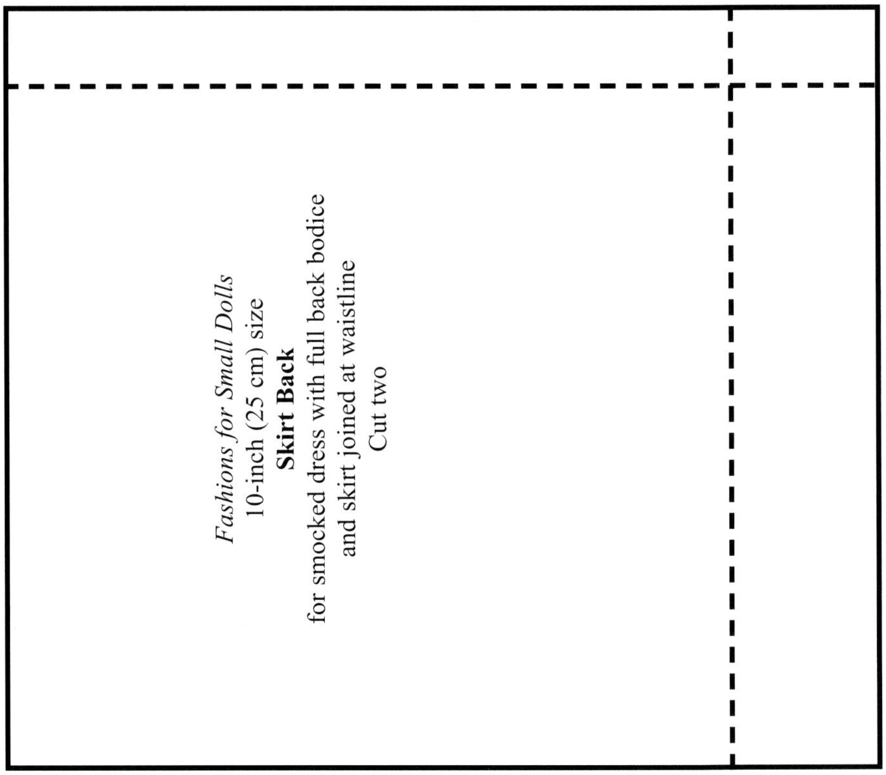

Fashions for Small Dolls
10-inch (25 cm) size
Skirt Back
for smocked dress with full back bodice
and skirt joined at waistline
Cut two

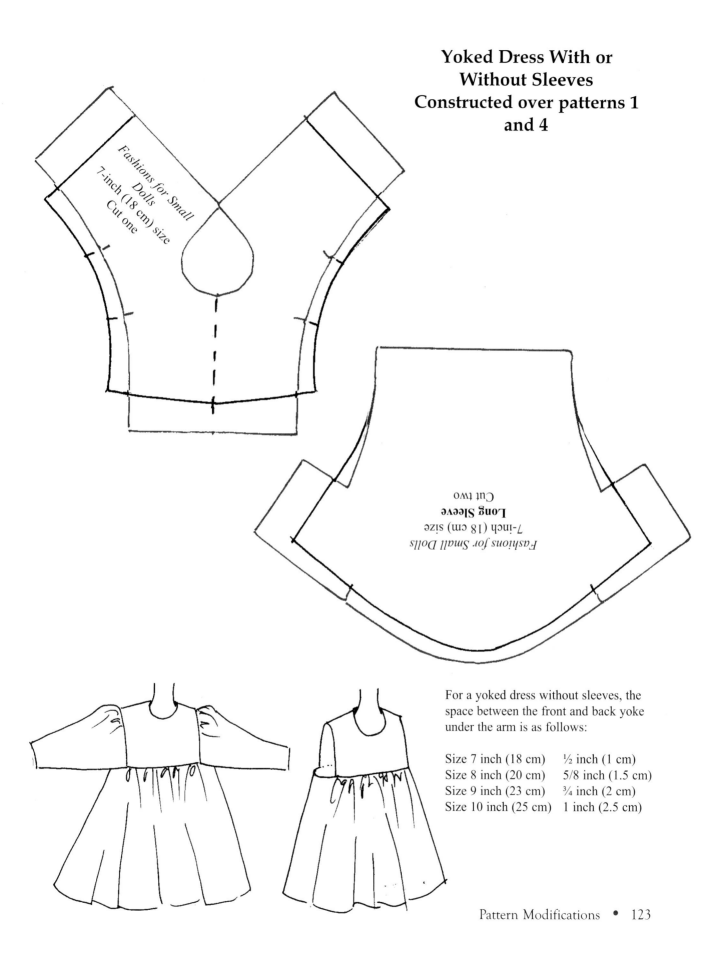

Yoked Dress With or Without Sleeves Constructed over patterns 1 and 4

Fashions for Small Dolls
7-inch (18 cm) size
Cut one

Fashions for Small Dolls
7-inch (18 cm) size
Long Sleeve
Cut two

For a yoked dress without sleeves, the space between the front and back yoke under the arm is as follows:

Size 7 inch (18 cm)   ½ inch (1 cm)
Size 8 inch (20 cm)   5/8 inch (1.5 cm)
Size 9 inch (23 cm)   ¾ inch (2 cm)
Size 10 inch (25 cm)   1 inch (2.5 cm)

Yokes of Different Styles
for a Jumper or Dress With
Back Closure

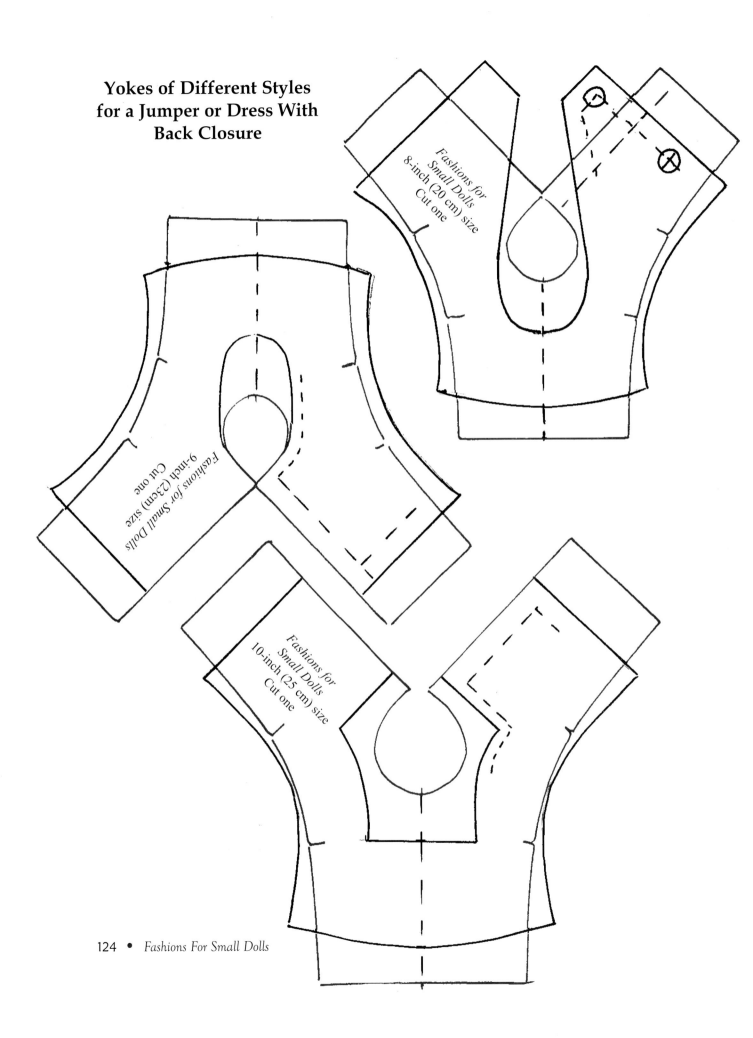

Fashions for
Small Dolls
8-inch (20 cm) size
Cut one

Fashions for Small Dolls
9-inch (23cm) size
Cut one

Fashions for
Small Dolls
10-inch (25 cm) size
Cut one

Sleeveless Bodice Made From Patterns 1 or 2

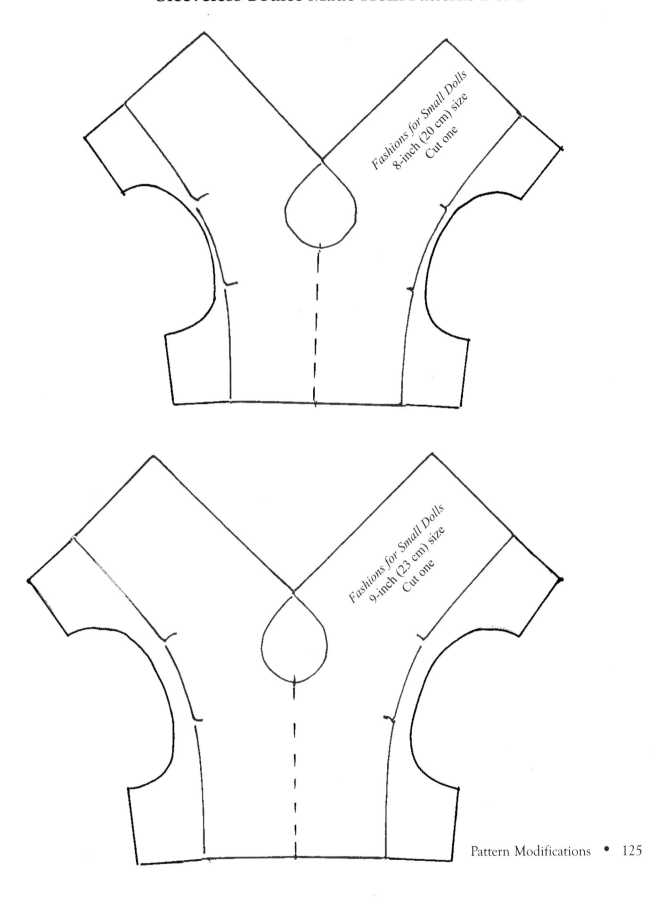

Fashions for Small Dolls
8-inch (20 cm) size
Cut one

Fashions for Small Dolls
9-inch (23 cm) size
Cut one

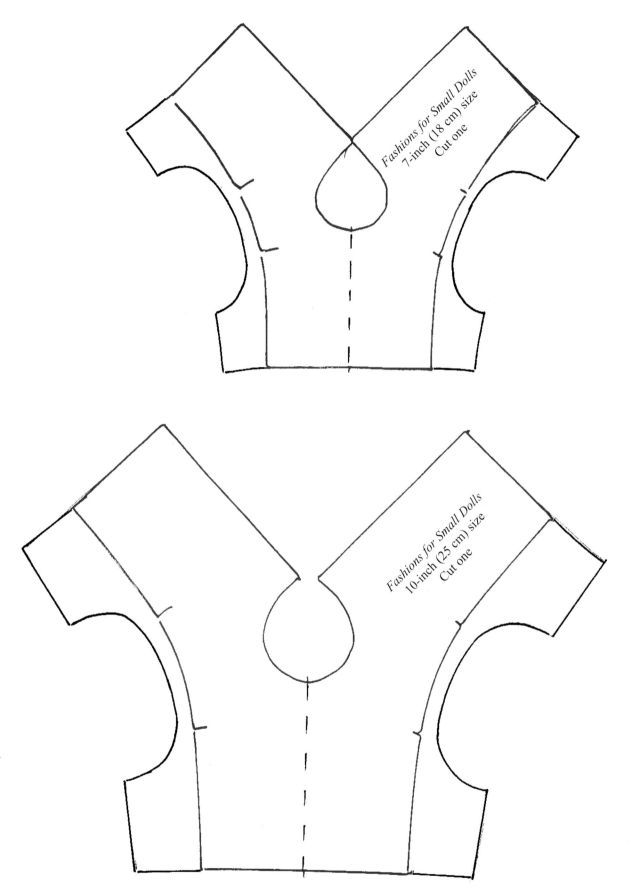

Fashions for Small Dolls
7-inch (18 cm) size
Cut one

Fashions for Small Dolls
10-inch (25 cm) size
Cut one

Long Pants Made Using Pattern 11

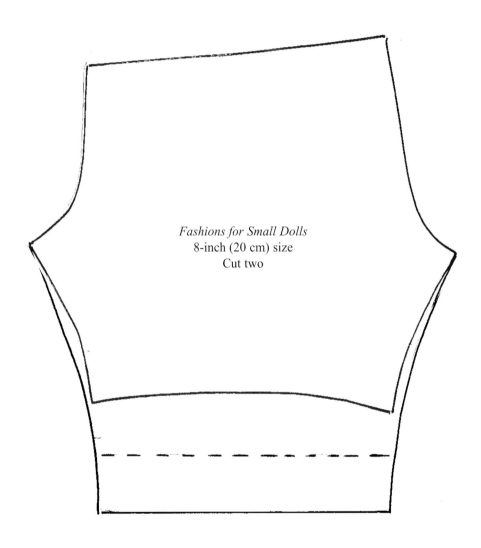

Fashions for Small Dolls
8-inch (20 cm) size
Cut two

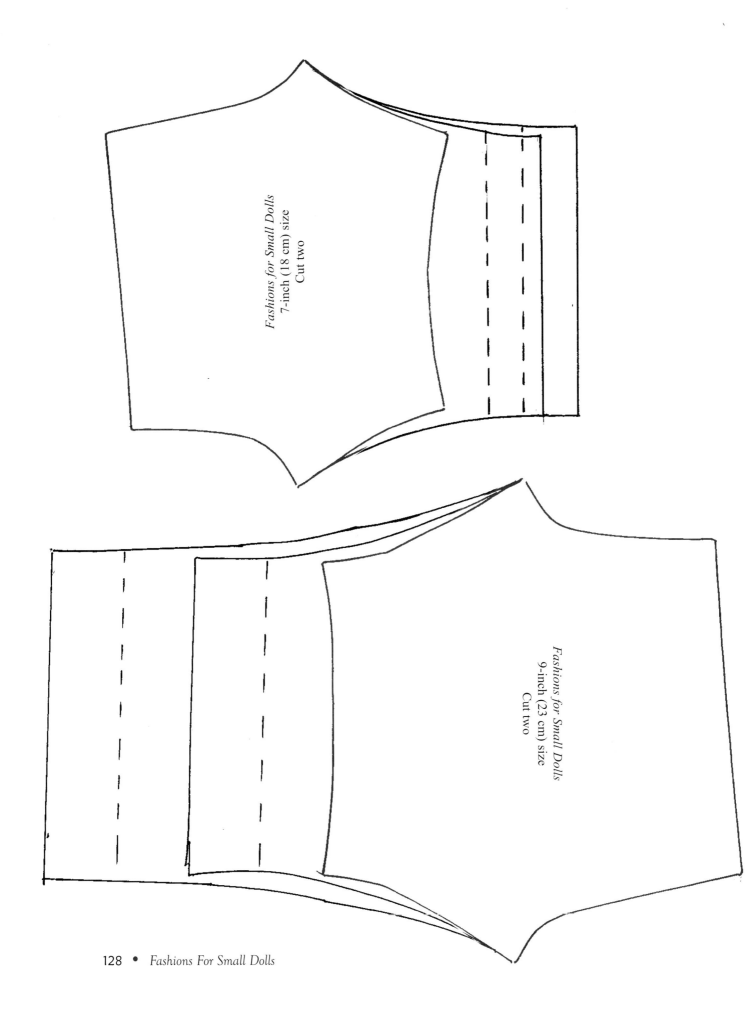

Fashions for Small Dolls
7-inch (18 cm) size
Cut two

Fashions for Small Dolls
9-inch (23 cm) size
Cut two

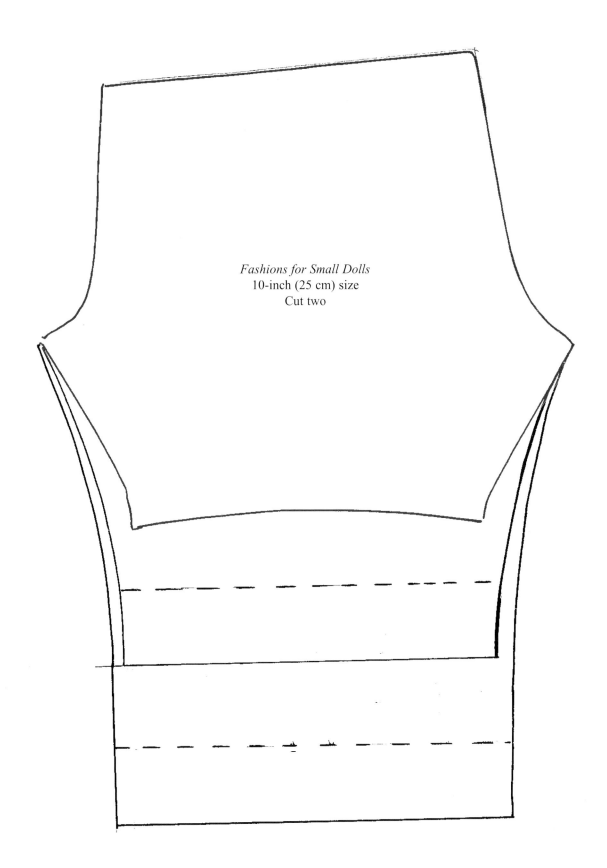

Fashions for Small Dolls
10-inch (25 cm) size
Cut two

Apron Top Using an Altered Pattern 1

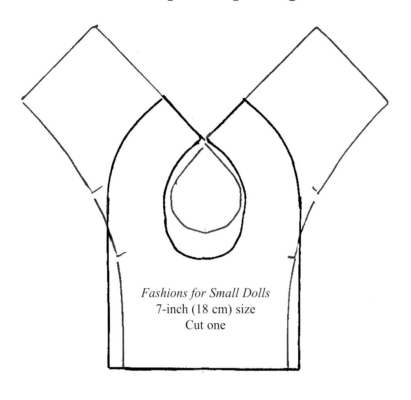

Fashions for Small Dolls
7-inch (18 cm) size
Cut one

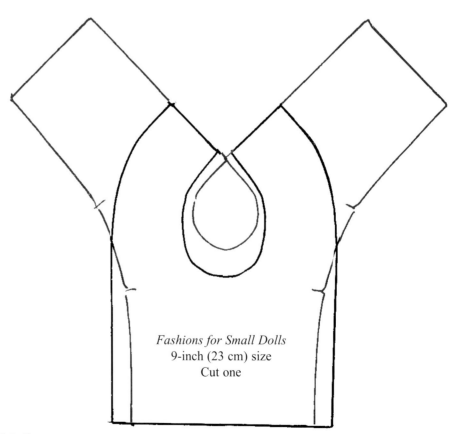

Fashions for Small Dolls
9-inch (23 cm) size
Cut one

Fashions for Small Dolls
8-inch (20 cm) size
Cut one

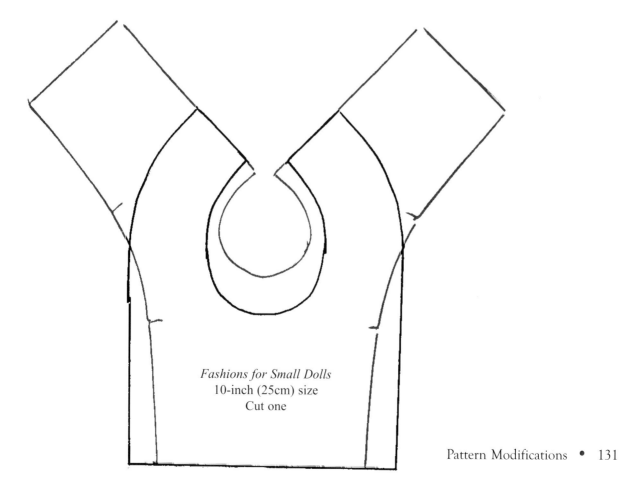

Fashions for Small Dolls
10-inch (25cm) size
Cut one

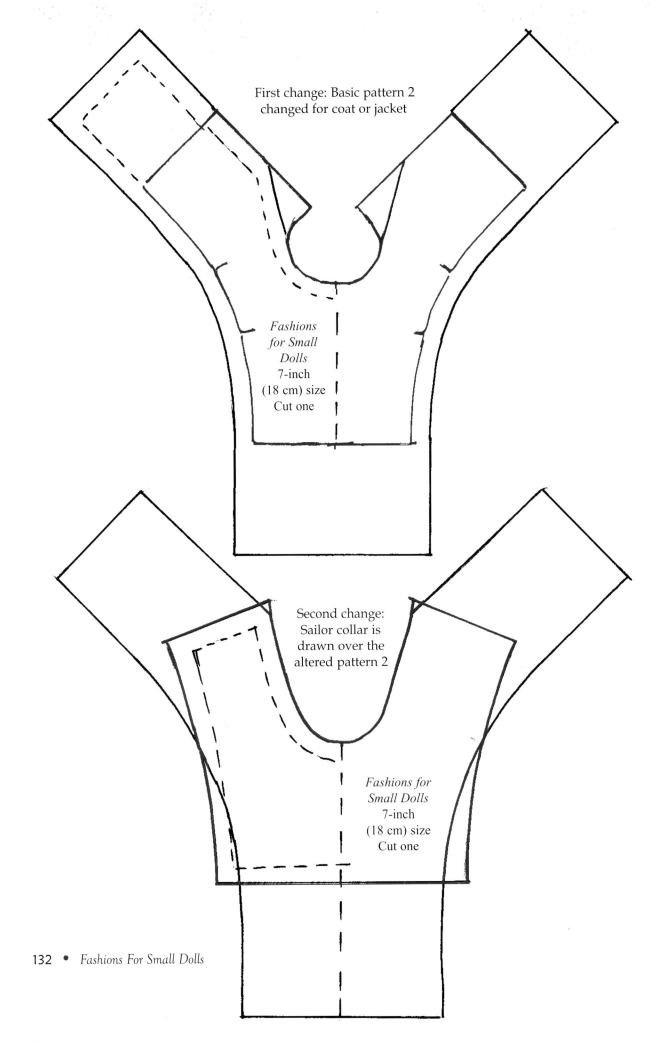

First change: Basic pattern 2
changed for coat or jacket

*Fashions
for Small
Dolls*
7-inch
(18 cm) size
Cut one

Second change:
Sailor collar is
drawn over the
altered pattern 2

*Fashions for
Small Dolls*
7-inch
(18 cm) size
Cut one

Blouse With Short Sleeves and Gathering at the Neck, Made with Pattern 8

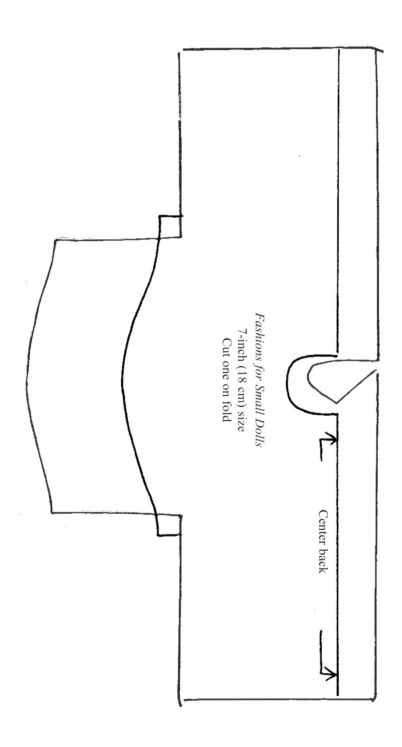

Fashions for Small Dolls
7-inch (18 cm) size
Cut one on fold

Center back

Short Jacket Constructed Using Pattern 8

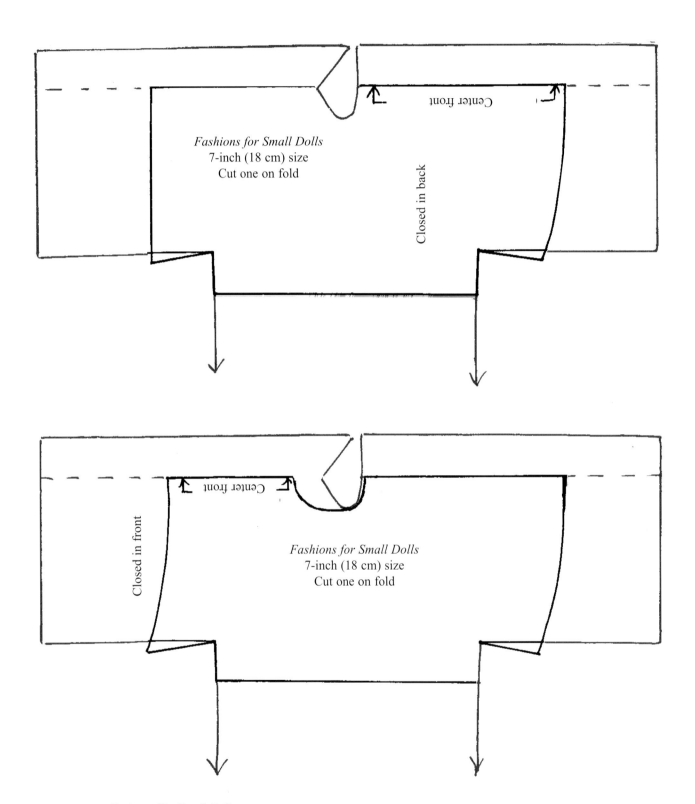

Fashions for Small Dolls
7-inch (18 cm) size
Cut one on fold

Center front

Closed in back

Fashions for Small Dolls
7-inch (18 cm) size
Cut one on fold

Center front

Closed in front

Dress Without Sleeves and a Long Bodice

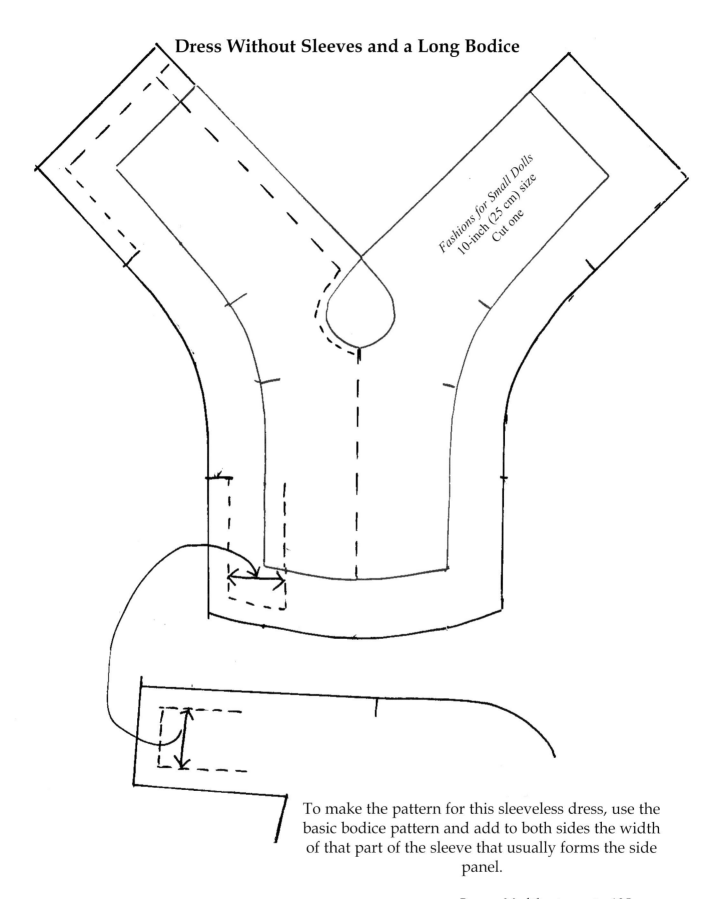

Fashions for Small Dolls
10-inch (25 cm) size
Cut one

To make the pattern for this sleeveless dress, use the basic bodice pattern and add to both sides the width of that part of the sleeve that usually forms the side panel.

Vest Constructed by Using Pattern 2

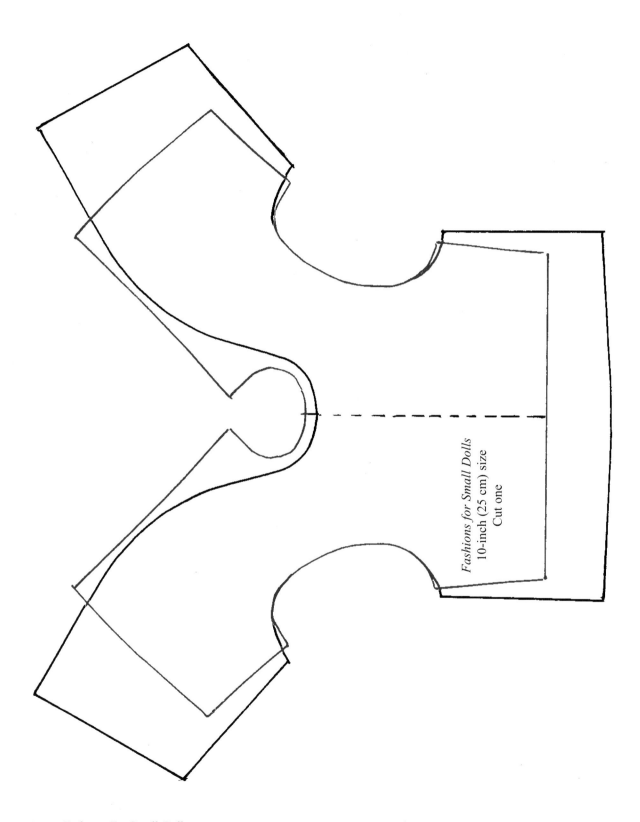

Fashions for Small Dolls
10-inch (25 cm) size
Cut one

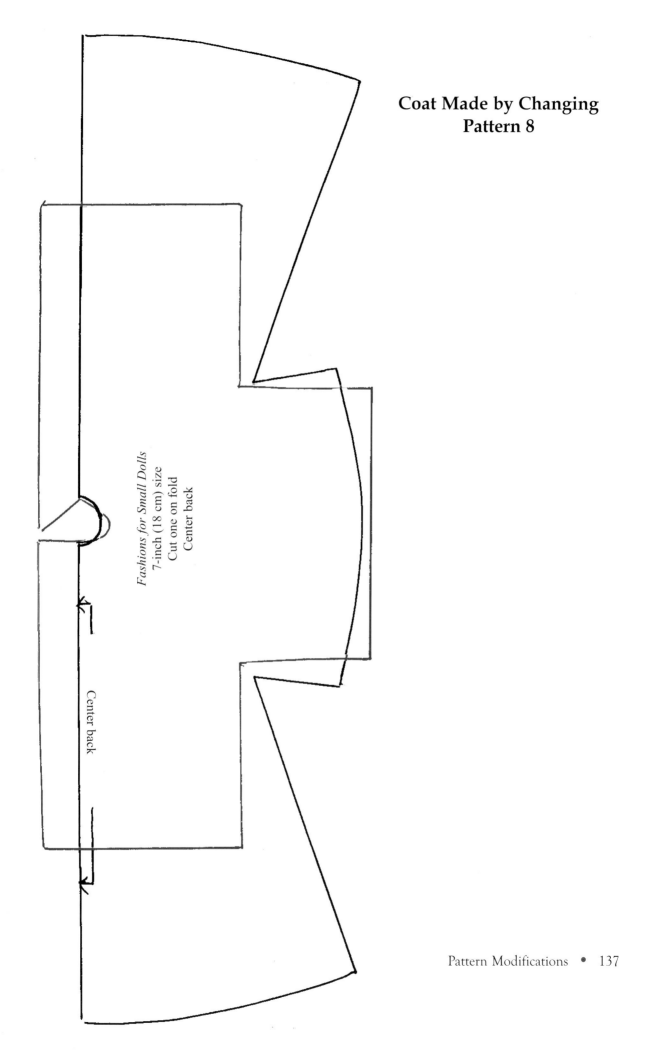

Coat Made by Changing Pattern 8

Fashions for Small Dolls
7-inch (18 cm) size
Cut one on fold
Center back

Center back

Coat Made by Altering Patterns 2 and 6

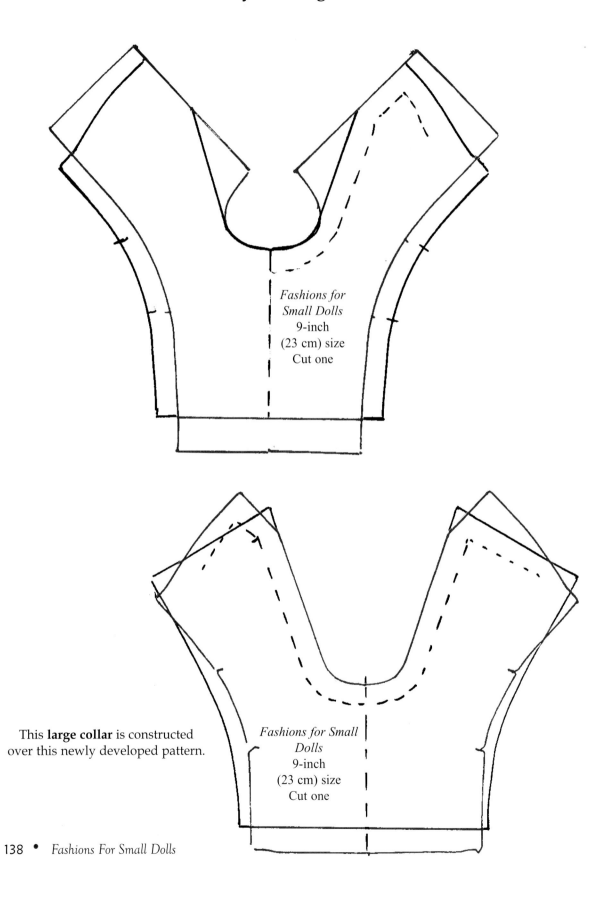

Fashions for Small Dolls
9-inch
(23 cm) size
Cut one

This **large collar** is constructed over this newly developed pattern.

Fashions for Small Dolls
9-inch
(23 cm) size
Cut one

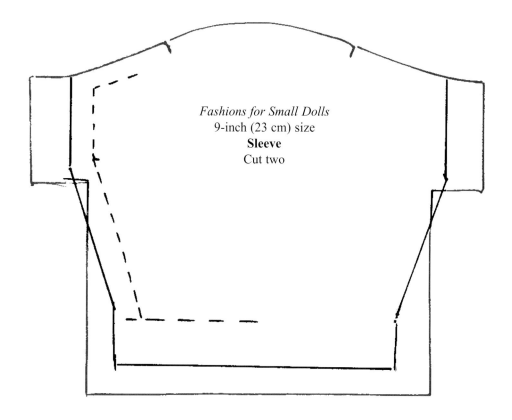

Fashions for Small Dolls
9-inch (23 cm) size
Sleeve
Cut two

Coat Made by Altering Patterns 2 and 4

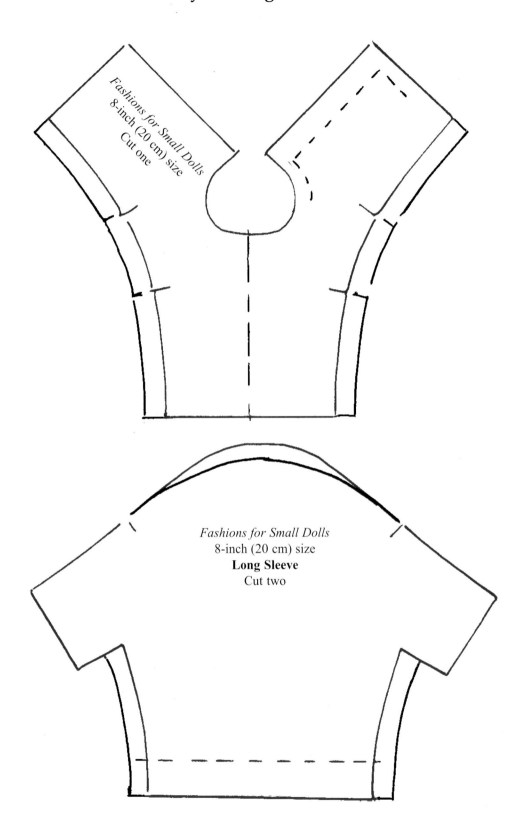

Fashions for Small Dolls
8-inch (20 cm) size
Cut one

Fashions for Small Dolls
8-inch (20 cm) size
Long Sleeve
Cut two

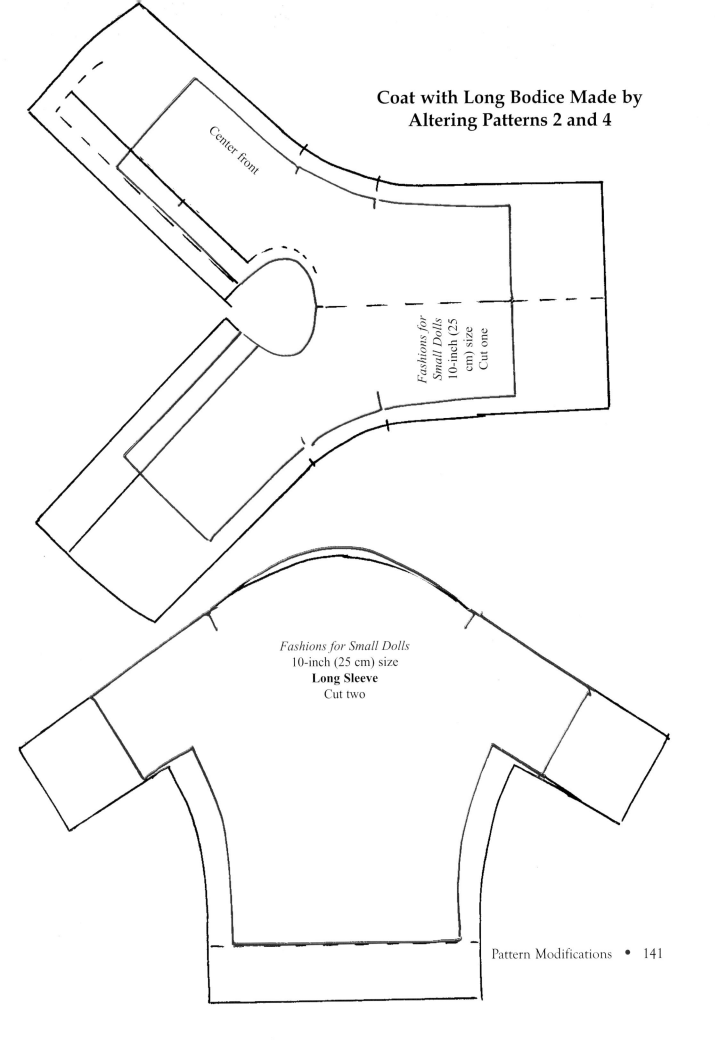

Coat with Long Bodice Made by Altering Patterns 2 and 4

Center front

Fashions for Small Dolls
10-inch (25 cm) size
Cut one

Fashions for Small Dolls
10-inch (25 cm) size
Long Sleeve
Cut two

Construction of One-half Circle Skirt

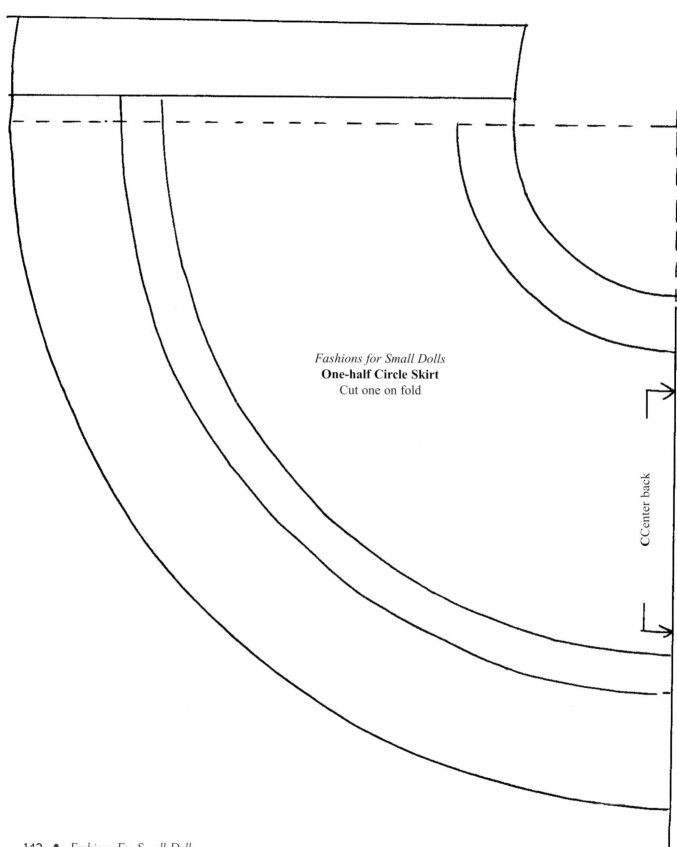

Fashions for Small Dolls
One-half Circle Skirt
Cut one on fold

CCenter back

Construction of One-fourth Circle Skirt

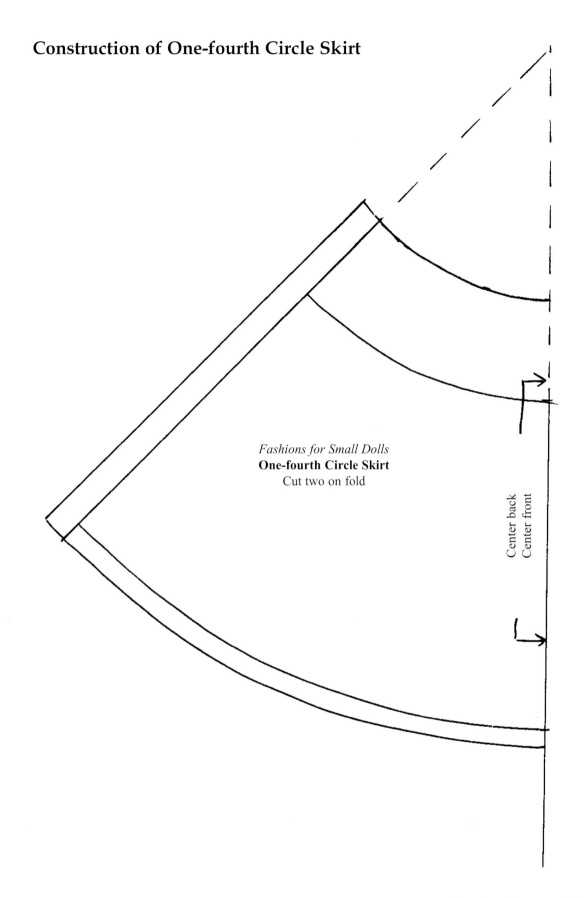

Fashions for Small Dolls
One-fourth Circle Skirt
Cut two on fold

Center back
Center front

About the Author

This is the second pattern book by Rosemarie Ionker. Her first, *A Closetful of Doll Clothes*, was also published by Portfolio Press.

A German national, Rosemarie Ionker (nee Meyer) was born on November 30, 1939, in Spremberg. She grew up in Cologne and Hamburg. After completing her secondary education, she went to art school in Cologne and then on to Hamburg's Institute of Fashion, from which she received a master's degree in dressmaking.

After graduation, she ran her own "Salon" and held fashion shows in a number of Germany cities, including Berlin and Hamburg. She was also an independent designer for garment production houses.

In 1965, after her marriage at age 26, Mrs. Ionker moved to Asia to join her husband, who was working for the Singer Company. The couple lived in Taiwan, Hong Kong, Indonesia and Singapore. While in Hong Kong, she started a children's fashion workshop, selling her creations there and expanding her market into Singapore and South Africa.

Later, while living in Indonesia, Mrs. Ionker added dolls' dresses, primarily smocked and embroidered models for collectors' dolls, to her stock. This enterprise was begun as a social project to teach sewing, smocking and embroidery work to young women who were often second or third wives (Indonesia is primarily a Muslim country, and men of Muslim faith are allowed to have more than one wife).

When Mrs. Ionker's father offered to take to Germany samples of the dolls' dresses the women were making, she decided to turn the project into a business under the name of "Petites Creations." What began as a small workshop had grown to a sizable business by the time she returned to Europe in 1987. She lived first in Switzerland and finally settled in Germany.

Over the past twenty years, Mrs. Ionker has gained much experience in making fashions for dolls. She has created outfits for dolls by some of the world's top artists, and has added hats, shoes, luggage and other accessories to her Petites Creations line of doll fashions. She also has raised three children, who now live in such diverse places as Bali and Germany.

Mrs. Ionker's know-how in making fashions for miniature dolls up to children's sizes is extensive. Her strong background in the history of clothing as well as fashion and her love of handwork, especially smocking and embroidery, are very apparent in her designs.